I0150939

THE
CANADIAN CONSTITUTION IN FORM AND IN FACT

BY

THE HONOURABLE

WILLIAM RENWICK RIDDELL, LL.D., F.R.S.C.

Justice of the Supreme Court of Ontario

Ἐλεύθερός ἐστιν ὁ ζῶν ὡς βούλεται.   EPICTETUS

Civitas ea autem in libertate est posita, quae suis stat viribus, non ex alieno arbitrio pendet.   LIVY

If you ask me what a free government is, I answer that it is what the people think so, and that they and not I are the natural, lawful and competent judges of the matter.   BURKE

THE LAWBOOK EXCHANGE, LTD.
Clark, New Jersey

ISBN 978-1-58477-962-9 (hardcover)
ISBN 978-1-61619-472-7 (paperback)

Lawbook Exchange edition 2015

The quality of this reprint is equivalent to the quality of the original work.

THE LAWBOOK EXCHANGE, LTD.
33 Terminal Avenue
Clark, New Jersey 07066-1321

*Please see our website for a selection of our other publications
and fine facsimile reprints of classic works of legal history:*
www.lawbookexchange.com

Library of Congress Cataloging-in-Publication Data

Riddell, William Renwick, 1852-1945.
  The Canadian constitution in form and in fact / by the
Honourable William Renwick Riddell.
      p. cm.
  Originally published: New York : Columbia University Press,
1923.
  Includes bibliographical references and index.
  ISBN-13: 978-1-58477-962-9 (cloth : alk. paper)
  ISBN-10: 1-58477-962-4 (cloth : alk. paper)
  1. Constitutional history--Canada. 2. Canada--Politics and
government. I. Title.
  KE4199.R53 2009
  342.7102'9--dc22
                                  2009003089

Printed in the United States of America on acid-free paper

COLUMBIA UNIVERSITY LECTURES

THE
CANADIAN CONSTITUTION IN FORM AND IN FACT

BY

THE HONOURABLE

WILLIAM RENWICK RIDDELL, LL.D., F.R.S.C.

Justice of the Supreme Court of Ontario

'Ελεύθερός ἐστιν ὁ ζῶν ὡς βούλεται.　　ΕPICTETUS

Civitas ea autem in libertate est posita, quae suis stat viribus, non ex alieno arbitrio pendet.　　LIVY

If you ask me what a free government is, I answer that it is what the people think so, and that they and not I are the natural, lawful and competent judges of the matter.　　BURKE

New York

COLUMBIA UNIVERSITY PRESS

1923

All rights reserved

COPYRIGHT, 1923,

By COLUMBIA UNIVERSITY PRESS

———

Set up and electrotyped.   Published September, 1923

TO

DEAN HARLAN F. STONE

AND THE FACULTY OF THE SCHOOL OF LAW

COLUMBIA UNIVERSITY

IN THE CITY OF NEW YORK

THESE LECTURES ARE DEDICATED

AS SOME SLIGHT RECOGNITION

OF THEIR KINDNESS TO

THE AUTHOR

PREFACE

These four lectures delivered in Kent Hall in Columbia University in the City of New York, April and May, 1923, are intended to explain in some detail the actual as compared with the apparent Constitution of Canada.

It is hoped that they may in some degree show the real democracy underlying the traditional and external monarchical form of government.

I have thought it well to confine myself in the text to somewhat general statements, reserving particulars and illustrations for the notes—which thus become rather longer and more comprehensive than is usual.

I have avoided, in great measure, drawing comparisons between the Constitution of the United States and that of Canada: it is an interesting and useful task to trace and discriminate the different methods by which two free peoples living side by side have solved their common problem of freedom combined with obedience to law—the strong temptation to enter upon this field, I have been occasionally unable to resist.

It may not be quite wise with the poet to say

> For forms of government let fools contest
> That which is best administered is best;

but it is certainly true that the happiness and liberty of a people do not depend upon the form—"the letter killeth, but the spirit giveth life."

Being wholly convinced that the future of the world and of our civilization depends upon the harmonious thought, speech and action of the great English-speaking peoples—and that a thorough knowledge of each other as well in their government as in their business and daily walk and conversation would be of advantage to all, I offer these lectures to my brethren of the United States.

Ne quaeso sit jurgium inter me et se—fratres enim sumus.

WILLIAM RENWICK RIDDELL

Osgoode Hall, Toronto, May 14, 1923.

NOTE

Those who desire a more extended and intimate knowledge of the Constitution of Canada would do well to consult:

Todd's *Parliamentary Government in the British Colonies*, 2nd Edition, London, Longmans, Green & Co., 1894

Bourinot's *Parliamentary Procedure and Practice in Canada*, 4th Edition, Toronto, Canada Law Book Company, 1916

Bourinot's *Manual of the Constitutional History of Canada*, New Edition, Toronto, The Copp, Clark Company, Ltd., 1901

Clement's *The Law of the Canadian Constitution*, 3rd Edition, Toronto, The Carswell Company, Ltd., 1916

Cameron's *The Canadian Constitution*, Winnipeg, Butterworth & Co. (Canada), Ltd., 1915

Lefroy's *A Short Treatise on Canadian Constitutional Law*, Toronto, The Carswell Company, Ltd., 1918 (with Professor W. P. M. Kennedy's Historical Note)

Lefroy's *The Law of Legislative Power in Canada*, Toronto, The Toronto Law Book and Publishing Co., 1897–8

Egerton and Grant's *Canadian Constitutional Development*, Toronto, The Musson Book Co., Ltd., 1907 (?)

Lefroy's *Leading Cases in Canadian Constitutional Law*, McWilliams' (2nd) Edition, Toronto, The Carswell Co., Ltd., 1920

Teece's *A Comparison Between the Federal Constitution of Canada and Australia*, Sydney, N. E. Smith, Ltd., 1902

Kennedy's *Documents of the Canadian Constitution*, Toronto, Oxford University Press, 1918

Kennedy's *The Constitution of Canada*, Oxford University Press, 1922

Riddell's *The Constitution of Canada in its History and Practical Working* (Dodge Lectures, Yale University), New Haven, Yale University Press, 1917

Borden's *Canadian Constitutional Studies*, University of Toronto Press, 1922

Smith's *Federalism in North America*, Boston, The Chapman Law Publishing Company, 1923

CONTENTS

CHAPTER   PAGE

   I. The Constitution   1
  II. The Executive and Legislature 17
 III. The Elected Legislative Houses 33
 IV. The Judicature 53
      Index 71

THE CONSTITUTION OF CANADA
IN FORM AND IN FACT

CHAPTER I

THE CONSTITUTION

The Dominion of Canada is composed of nine Provinces, one Territory (Yukon) and the "Northwest Territories".[1] The Provinces have substantially the same jurisdiction, rights and powers; while the Dominion has jurisdiction, rights and powers of its own.

In considering the Constitution of Canada, it must always be kept in mind that much is unwritten, with the result that much of what is written is or may be misleading. There is real danger of one who is accustomed to a written Constitution, misunderstanding the effect of the Statutes, etc., constituting the written part of the Constitution of Canada.

The word "Constitution" has a different connotation in American and in Canadian (i.e., British) usage. Speaking somewhat generally—in the United States, "the 'Constitution' is a written document containing so many letters, words and sentences, which authoritatively and without appeal dictates what shall and what shall not be done"; in Canada, the Constitution is "the totality of the principles more or less vaguely and generally stated upon which we think the people should be governed." In Canada anything unconstitutional is wrong, however legal it may be; in the United States anything unconstitutional is illegal, however right and even advisable it may be; in the United States anything unconstitutional is illegal, in Canada to say that a measure is unconstitutional rather suggests that it is legal, but inadvisable.[2]

WRITTEN CONSTITUTION

The Written Constitution of Canada is to be found in The British North America Act, 1867 (in citation usually contracted to "B. N. A. Act") and amending Acts.

The B. N. A. Act is in form and legal effect a Statute of the Imperial Parliament at Westminster; in fact, it is a contract agreed upon by Canadian statesmen and given legal validity by the Imperial Parliament.

For various reasons,[3] the former Provinces, Canada, Nova Scotia, New Brunswick, Prince Edward Island and Newfoundland, were dissatisfied with their condition; and after a conference in Charlottetown, P. E. I., of representative statesmen from the "Maritime Provinces," (which was visited by representatives from Canada), representatives from the five Provinces met in Quebec, in October, 1864, and passed Resolutions which formed the basis of the British North America Act, 1867.[4]

Prince Edward Island and Newfoundland declined to become part of the proposed confederation or Union; and the Act was drawn up and passed, forming Canada, Nova Scotia and New Brunswick into the "Dominion of Canada", with four separate Provinces. The Act provided for the admission of Newfoundland, Prince Edward Island and British Columbia into the Union, on an Address from the Parliament of Canada and the Legislature of the Province. The two latter have taken advantage of this provision, but Newfoundland still stands apart.[5]

AMENDMENTS TO THE WRITTEN CONSTITUTION
OF THE DOMINION

There is no provision in the B. N. A. Act for amendments thereto; the reason is historical.

The old Province of Lower Canada which expired as a legal entity in 1841 by the effect of the Union Act[6] which united the Provinces of Upper Canada and Lower Canada into the Province of Canada, was largely populated by French-Canadians almost all of whom were Catholic and much attached to their old law and customs; the remainder of the people of the new Dominion were largely English-speaking and Protestant, in general attached to English law and customs. While the French-Canadians were willing to enter into a contract with their English-speaking brethren, they were not willing to enter into a contract which could be varied by the more numerous English without their consent.

There is, however, no difficulty in having an Amendment made if and when desired. An Address to the Sovereign is passed by both Houses of Parliament at Ottawa asking for the Amendment specified. According to the unwritten Constitution, the vote on the Address must be unanimous (or practically unanimous) or it will not be forwarded to London. When the Address is received by the Colonial Secretary in London, the desired amendment to the B. N. A. Act is passed by the Imperial Parliament as of course and without debate. This is, in substance, simply giving legal validity to an amendment agreed upon by the parties to the original contract, which they desire to amend.[7]

AMENDMENTS TO THE CONSTITUTION OF THE PROVINCES

The scheme of Confederation being that there should be a number of Provinces, each with jurisdiction over matters of local concern, property, civil rights, etc., in the Province, and it being intended that the former Province of Lower Canada should be one of such Provinces, there was no objection on the part of the French-Canadians to allowing the Provinces to change their written Constitution in most particulars. One matter, however, it was agreed on all hands must be provided for—Canada was to remain British; she was not, however democraric, to become Republican. The Preamble to the B. N. A. Act expressly declares the undoubted fact that the desire of the Provinces was "to be federally united under the Crown of the United Kingdom"; and the Provinces were guaranteed against any change in this relationship, just as the Constitution of the United States guarantees to every State a republican form of government.[8]

The B. N. A. Act therefore provides that "in each Province, the Legislature may exclusively make laws in relation to . . . The Amendment from time to time . . . of the Constitution of the Province except as regards the office of the Lieutenant-Governor." While the Lieutenant-Governor of the Province is appointed by the Dominion, he directly represents the Sovereign in the Province, and his office, as at present constituted, is a guaranty of the Province remaining under the Crown of the United Kingdom and a part of the British Commonwealth.

Many changes have been made by the Provinces: Second Chambers have been abolished, leaving the Legislature with only one House; certain named persons have been declared members of the Legislative Assembly without election; the term of a Legislature has been extended by the Legislature itself, etc., etc.; but an attempt to give the people the power to make or repeal laws by direct vote by Initiative and Referendum proved futile, as the Courts held that this would interfere with the office of the Lieutenant-Governor who was the official head of the Legislature.[9]

LEGISLATIVE POWERS IN CANADA NOT DELEGATED

The legal conception of the powers of the Parliament of the Dominion and the Legislatures of the Provinces is that they are a grant by the Imperial Parliament through the B. N. A. Act and amending Acts. It might consequently be considered that these powers are delegated and are limited by the maxim, *Delegatus non potest delegare.* But that view has been authoritatively and definitely negatived. "It rests upon a mistaken view of . . . the nature and principles of legislation. The . . . Legislature has powers expressly limited by the Act of the Imperial Parliament which created it and it can, of course, do nothing beyond the limits which circumscribe these powers. But, when acting within those limits, it is not in any sense an agent or delegate of the Imperial Parliament, but has and was intended to have plenary powers of legislation as large and of the same nature as those of [the Imperial] Parliament itself." [10] And "the power . . . of [the Imperial] Parliament is so transcendent and absolute that it cannot be confined either for causes or persons, within any bounds. . . . It has sovereign and uncontrollable authority in the making, confirming, enlarging, restraining, abrogating, repealing, reviving and expounding of laws concerning matters of all possible denominations." [11] "In short, the Legislature within its jurisdiction can do everything that is not naturally impossible and is restrained by no rule, human or divine." [12]

In respect of Canada, the whole ambit of legislation concerning matters of all possible denominations in Canada is divided between the Dominion and the Provinces, as in the United States between the United States and the States: differing however from the rule in the United States, any subject not expressly allotted to the Provinces falls to the Dominion.

Speaking generally, the Provinces have jurisdiction in civil law and matters of a local or private nature, the Dominion in criminal law and matters of a general nature affecting the whole of Canada. [13]

There is nothing in the way of "Constitution Limitations" in Canada any more than there is in England: once the subject of legislation is found to be within the jurisdiction of Dominion or of Province, the power must be held to be absolute. When a question arises whether the prescribed limits have been exceeded, the Courts must of necessity determine that question by looking to the terms of the B. N. A. Act and amending Acts. If what has been done is legislation within the scope of the words giving the power, the Court must so decide; but it is not for any Court of Justice to inquire further.[14] Where there is jurisdiction over the subject matter, considerations of hardship or injustice have no weight.[15]

As the legislatures of the Dominion and the Provinces are not delegates, they may and often do intrust Commissioners with the exercise of their powers.[16]

NOTES TO CHAPTER I

[1]Of these, Nova Scotia and New Brunswick were separate Provinces before the coming into force, July 1, 1867, of the British North America Act (1867), 30, 31 Vict. C. 3, (Imp.). Ontario and Quebec from 1791, Canada or Constitutional Act, 31 Geo. III, C. 31 (Imp.), until 1841, The Union Act, (1840), 3, 4 Vict. C. 35 (Imp.), were separate Provinces as Upper Canada and Lower Canada, having been formed by the division into two parts of the old Province of Quebec which had been created by The Quebec Act (1774), 14 Geo. III, C. 83, (Imp.): that former Province of Quebec was an enlargement to the West and South of the original "Government" of Quebec (see the Royal Proclamation of October 7, 1763); but it had been seriously diminished in area *de facto* and more *de jure* by the Definitive Treaty of September 3, 1783. (*De jure* and *de facto* became one under "Jay's Treaty" of Amity, Commerce and Navigation, of November 19, 1794).

The original Dominion of Canada, formed July 1, 1867, by the B. N. A. Act, was composed of four Provinces, Ontario, Quebec, Nova Scotia and New Brunswick.

Manitoba became the fifth Province, being carved out of the immense Hudson Bay Territory bought by the Dominion in 1870 and formed into a Province by the Dominion Act of May 12, 1870, 33 Vict. C. 3, (Dom.).

In 1871, British Columbia became the sixth Province. It had been formed in 1866 by the union of the two provinces of British Columbia and Vancouver Island under the Act (1866) 29, 30 Vict. C. 67, (Imp.).

In 1873, Prince Edward Island became the seventh Province. Imperial Order-in-Council at Windsor, June 26, 1873.

In 1905, Alberta and Saskatchewan became the eighth and ninth Provinces, being formed from part of the Northwestern Territory, etc., by the Dominion Acts, (1905), 4, 5 Edw. VII, CC. 3 and 42, (Dom.).

The Yukon Territory bordering on Alaska was originally formed as the

"Yukon Judicial District" by the Proclamation of the Governor-in-Council (Dominion) of August 16, 1897; and became the Yukon Territory, June 18, 1898, under the Act, (1898), 61 Vict. C. 6, (Dom.).

All the remainder of Canada is "The Northwest Territories," (1905), 4, 5, Edw. VII, C. 27, (Dom.); (1906), R. S. C. C. 62, the District of Keewatin having disappeared under the Dominion Proclamation of July 24, 1905, authorized by the Act, R. S. C., (1887), C. 53, Sec. 3 (2), (Dom.).

[2] My own language in substance in "The Constitution of Canada in its History and Practical Working" (Dodge Lectures, Yale University) Yale University Press, 1917, p. 52. See Bell vs. Town of Burlington, (1915), 34 Ont. L. Rep., 619, at p. 622, per Riddell, J. (Appellate Division, Supreme Court of Ontario).

The American use of the word "constitutional," "unconstitutional," etc., is perhaps being more extensively followed by Canadian lawyers and statesmen by reason of the constant reference to American authorities: careful speakers and writers, however, use the terminology, *intra vires, ultra vires,* etc. It may assist an American to understand our use of the words "constitutional" and "unconstitutional" if he considers the "Electoral College." The Electoral College was expressly adopted to avoid the dangers of the election of the President of the United States by popular vote—the people would be led by a few active and designing men (Pinckney of South Carolina), the ignorance of the people would find it in the power of one set of men dispersed through the Union and acting in concert to delude the people into any appointment (Gerry of Massachusetts) and it would be as unnatural to refer the choice of Chief Magistrate to the people as it would be to refer a trial of colour to a blind man (Mason of Virginia). Accordingly, it was decided that the election of the President should be placed in the hands of a select body of gentlemen; in theory, these gentlemen were to exercise an independent judgment as to the best man for the position. The nation was to trust to their impartiality, integrity, intelligence and patriotism to make the best choice possible; and naturally their character, their independence of partyism and faction, their judgment and candor were all important. We know the fact; we know that the personality of the elector does not count; we know in advance how the elector will vote; as soon as we know who the electors are, we know who is to be the President.

No one doubts that if the Electoral College in 1912 had elected Mr. Taft, the election would have been legal and "constitutional" in the United States sense, but it would have been "unconstitutional" in the Canadian (British) sense. "It isn't done." See a paper "The Second President Lincoln," Trans. Royal Society of Canada, Vol. 15, 3rd Series, 1921, section II, pp. 135, sqq.

[3] The "Trent Affair" of 1861 showed a possibility of trouble with the United States; the agitation for the revocation of the Elgin-Marcy Reciprocity Treaty of 1854 indicated the necessity of the trade routes being east and west instead of north and south; there was no little truculence amongst certain classes in the United States toward Britain during and succeeding the Civil War, and some politicians urged the acquisition of Canada— "Annexation";—it may be remembered that the Fenian Invasions of 1866

and 1867 were from the United States, and that General Grant said that if Sherman could not conquer Canada in thirty days, he should lose his commission—the Provinces felt the need of a common defence and a common trade policy without hampering inter-provincial custom houses; the Province of Canada was distracted over the question of representation in Parliament of the two parts, Upper Canada or Canada West (afterwards Ontario) and Lower Canada or Canada East (afterwards Quebec); the Maritime Provinces wanted railway connection with the west and Canada with the east. Such were some of the moving influences which brought about Confederation.

⁴"The B. N. A. Act . . . should be viewed as a Treaty" (Lord Carnarvon). There was no change made at Westminster in the Bill drawn up by the Colonial representatives. Stanley, the Colonial Secretary, indeed suggested that the term "Kingdom of Canada" intended to be used, might be unpalatable to the United States, and the term "Dominion of Canada" was substituted to avoid hurting the supposed susceptibilities of our neighbours to the south. The word "Dominion" was adopted from Psalms, 72, 8—"dominion from sea to sea and from the river unto the ends of the earth," an aspiration and a prophecy.

⁵What was actually done was that the authorities of the Dominion and of the Province arranged terms by negotiation, the Parliaments passed an Address to the Queen, and thereupon the "Queen by and with the advice of Her Majesty's Most Honourable Privy Council" passed an order in Council "to admit the Province into the Union . . . on such terms and conditions in each case as are in the addresses expressed and as the Queen thinks fit to approve," B. N. A. Act (1867), C. 146—all this was mere matter of routine except the negotiation of the terms by Dominion and Province.

⁶The Union Act, (1840), 3, 4, Vict. C. 35, (Imp.) by section 1, empowered Her Majesty to declare or to authorize the Governor-General of the two Provinces of Upper Canada and Lower Canada to declare that the two Provinces from and after a certain day to be stated in the Proclamation, should form and constitute one Province, called the Province of Canada. The Act was assented to, July 23, 1840; the Queen, with the advice of Her Privy Council (in other words, the Imperial Government) on August 10, 1840, authorized the Governor-General to declare by Proclamation that the two Provinces should form and be one Province; Lord Sydenham, the Governor-General, by Proclamation dated February 3, 1841, fixed February 7, 1841, for the Union.

Thereafter until July 1, 1867, there was the one Province of Canada; but each part had géographically and for many purposes a separate name, i.e., Upper Canada or Canada West and Lower Canada or Canada East.

⁷There have been a number of Amendments to the B. N. A. Act of more or less importance: it may be of interest to mention them.

1869,

1—When Canada bought the enormous Rupert's Land from the Hudson Bay Company for £300,000, the Imperial Treasury was asked to guarantee the loan to be effected by Canada for paying the Company; and agreed to do so on condition that the sum should be a first charge on the Consolidated

Revenue Fund of Canada. This was agreed to, and the Imperial Parliament passed an Act to prevent the Dominion by any Statute impairing such priority, (1869) 32, 33 Vict. C. 101 (Imp.).

This limitation of the powers of the Dominion was for financial reasons for a temporary purpose, and is not of consequence.

1870,

2—A similar Act was passed in 1870 in respect of the guaranty by the Imperial Treasury of £1,100,000 to be borrowed for the construction of fortifications, (1870) 33, 34 Vict. C. 82 (Imp.). (A similar Act was passed in 1892, 55, 56 Vict. C. 32 (Imp.), when the Imperial Treasury had agreed to loan up to £150,000 to enable the Province of British Columbia to settle "crofters" from Scotland in that Province, the Province to repay the loan by debentures charged upon the Revenues of the Province. Section 4 of this Act prevented the Province impairing the validity or priority of this charge without the consent of the Treasury).

1871,

3—In 1871, an Act was passed to remove the doubt that had arisen in respect to the power of the Dominion to establish Provinces and to provide for the representation of such Provinces. (1871) 34 Vict. C. 28, (Imp.). (The Act also declared valid certain statutes of the Dominion as to Rupert's Land and Manitoba.)

1875,

4—Doubts having arisen as to the privileges, immunities and powers of the Canadian Houses of Parliament and the members thereof, an Act was passed in 1875 to remove such doubts. (1875) 38, 39 Vict. C. 38, (Imp.).

1895,

5—The Parliament of Canada in 1894 passed an Act, 57, 58 Vict. C. 11, (Dom.), providing for the appointment of a Deputy Speaker of the Senate during the absence or illness of the Speaker; but in view of the provision in the B. N. A. Act, sec. 34, for the appointment of a Speaker only, there was doubt expressed as to the power to appoint a Deputy; and the Canadian Act contained a provision, sec. 4, that it should "not come into force until Her Majesty's pleasure thereon has been signified by proclamation in the Canada Gazette." Thereupon was passed the Act (1895) 59 Vict. C. 3, (Imp.), to remove such doubt; and the Canadian Act came into force.

1907,

6—The B. N. A. Act, secs. 118, 119, provides for certain yearly payments by the Dominion to the original four Provinces; and there were, *dehors* the B. N. A. Act, provisions for paying certain sums annually to the other Provinces; the Provinces complained of the inadequacy of such payments, and after considerable agitation and negotiation, another basis of payment was arrived at. An Act was thereupon passed, (1907), 7 Edw. VII, C. 11 (Imp.), providing for grants on the new basis.

1915,

7—The B. N. A. Act, sec. 21, provides for 72 Senators; the number was increased on the admission of new Provinces into the Union, and a readjustment became advisable. Moreover the provision in the B. N. A. Act, sec. 51, for the decennial readjustment according to population of the representation in the House of Commons was found to work a hardship in a small Province with practically stationary population. An Act was accordingly passed, (1915) 5, 6, Geo. V, C. 45, (Imp.), fixing the number of Senators and providing that each Province should have at least as many members of the House of Commons as it had Senators.

1916,

8—The B. N. A. Act, sec. 30, provides that "Every House of Commons shall continue for five years . . . and no longer"; all parties in 1915 when the War was raging, agreed that it would not be well to have a General Election at that time; and both Houses of Parliament at Ottawa presented an Address, passed unanimously, to the King to have the term of the existing Parliament extended; otherwise, under the provisions of sec. 50 of the B. N. A. Act there must be an election. Accordingly the Act (1916) 6, 7, Geo. V, C. 19 (Imp.) was passed, June 1, 1916, extending the term of the existing Parliament until October 7, 1917. At the next sittings of the Canadian Parliament, a Resolution was introduced into the House of Commons at Ottawa by the Government for an Address asking another extension; but while the Government had a majority, 82 to 62, there was a substantial minority; and the matter was dropped, Sir Robert Borden, the then Prime Minister, saying that in the absence of "unanimity or practical unanimity", the resolution should not be acted upon. Accordingly there was a General Election in 1917.

Of these Amendments it will be observed Nos. 1, 2 and 8, were for a temporary purpose and have no lasting effect; Nos. 3, 4, and 5, are rather declaratory than amending; No. 6 carried into effect a financial arrangement between the Dominion and the Provinces, and No. 7 gives legal validity to a scheme for representation, etc., determined upon in the Dominion. Only No. 7 is really a "Constitutional Amendment" in any practical sense.

[8] Constitution of the United States, article IV, section 4 "The United States shall guarantee to every State in this Union, a Republican Form of Government. . ."

[9] Prince Edward Island, coming into the Dominion in 1873 with two Houses, abolished her Legislative Council in the same year; Manitoba, formed in 1870 with two Houses, abolished her Legislative Council in 1876; New Brunswick, one of the original four Provinces of the Dominion in 1867 with two Houses, abolished her Legislative Council in 1891. There are but two Provinces now with two Houses, viz., Nova Scotia and Quebec: Ontario, Alberta and Saskatchewan never had a Second Chamber, and British Columbia abolished hers in 1871 before entering the Dominion.

In 1918, the Legislature of Ontario passed an Act, 8 Geo. V, C. 4, (Ont.), continuing its own life until it should have held one session after the close of the war. One member of the Assembly spoke against the extension on the ground that it was unconstitutional; and beyond question such an Act would be unconstitutional in our sense in the absence of extraordinary circumstances: it never would be unconstitutional in the American sense of the word. (This was much like legislation in Britain and in Newfoundland, (1918)

8, 9 Geo. V, C. 2, (Nfld.).) In Britain the maximum duration of a Parliament was in 1715 fixed at seven years by the Act, 1 Geo. I, Stat. 2, C. 38, (Imp.); this term was shortened to five years by the Act (1911), 1, 2 Geo. V, C. 13, (Imp.). During the war, Parliament extended its own life to five years and eight months by the Act, (1915) 5, 6, Geo. V, C. 100, (Imp.); then to six years and three months, (1916), 6, 7, Geo. V, C. 44, (Imp.), and the following year to six years and ten months, (1917), 7 Geo. V, C. 13, (Imp.). It must be remembered that this Parliament had been elected under the Act of 1911 for five years as a maximum.

Alberta by the Act of 1917, C. 38, (Alta.), enacted that twelve of the members of the Legislative Assembly named who had enlisted for Overseas Service should be members of the next Legislative Assembly for the Constituencies which they represented in the existing Assembly.

The Act mentioned in the Text as having been held *ultra vires* ("unconstitutional" in the American sense of the word) was "The Initiative and Referendum Act" of Manitoba, (1916), 6 Geo. V, C. 59, (Man.); it provides that a proposed law may be submitted in a Petition to the Legislative Assembly of electors not less in number than eight per cent of the number of the votes polled at the last election; unless this law be enacted by the Assembly in the same Session substantially as submitted, it must be submitted to a vote of the electors at the next General Election (unless a special Referendum vote be asked for in the Petition, in which case the vote is usually to be taken within six months of the presentation of the Petition). If approved by the vote, it becomes law within 30 days subject to the powers of veto and disallowance provided in the B. N. A. Act. A number of electors equivalent to not less than five per cent of the number of votes at the last election may petition for the repeal of any law, and much the same process may then be gone through. There are also certain provisions not of importance here.

The Court of Appeal of Manitoba, reversing the *pro formâ* judgment of the Chief Justice of the King's Bench, held this legislation *ultra vires* of the Province; re The Initiative and Referendum Act (1916) 27 Man. L. R., 1; and this decision was affirmed by the Judicial Committee of the Privy Council, (1919) A. C., 935, on the ground that the Act "would compel the Lieutenant-Governor to submit the proposed law to a body totally distinct from the legislature of which he is the constitutional head, and would render him powerless to prevent it from becoming an actual law if approved by those voters."

[10] I use the words of Lord Selborne, Lord Chancellor, giving the judgment of the Judicial Committee of the Privy Council in The Queen v. Burah, (1878), 3 A. C. 889, at p. 904. This was a case concerning the powers of the Legislature of India created by the Act, (1861), 24, 25 Vict. C. 67 (Imp.). The doctrine that the Colonial Legislature is a delegate of the Imperial Legislature had some currency at one time, but it has been put an end to by The Queen v. Burah and Hodge v. The Queen, (1883), 9 A. C. 117; see Powell v. Apollo Candle Company, (1885), 10 A. C. 282, at p. 290.

I said in Smith v. City of London, (1909), 20 Ont. Law Rep., 133, at p. 137: "The powers of the Legislature . . . are the same in intension though not in extension as those of the Imperial Parliament; the Legislature is limited in the territory in which it may legislate and in the subjects, the Imperial Parliament is not; that is the whole difference."

[11] Blackstone's Commentaries, Book 1, p. 160.

[12] The language is my own in giving judgment in Florence Mining Co., Ltd., v. Cobalt Lake Mining Co., Ltd., (1908), 18 Ont. Law Rep., 275, at p. 279; my judgment was affirmed by the Court of Appeal, (1908) 18 Ont. Law Rep. 282, and the Judicial Committee of the Privy Council, (1910) 43 Ont. Law Rep. 474; 102 L. T., N. S., 375.

DeLolme, "The Constitution of England," new ed., Hatchard, London, 1834, p. 117 (n), says: "It is a fundamental principle with the English lawyers that Parliament can do everything except making a woman a man, and a man a woman." "An Act of Parliament can do no wrong, though it may do several things that look pretty odd," says Sir John Holt, C. J., in City of London v. Wood, (1700), 12 Mod., 669, at pp. 687, 688.

[13] The B. N. A. Act by sections 91 and 92 divides the field of legislation thus:

"91. It shall be lawful for the Queen, by and with the advice and consent of the Senate and House of Commons, to make laws for the peace, order, and good government of Canada, in relation to all matters not coming within the classes of subjects by this Act assigned exclusively to the Legislatures of the Provinces; and for greater certainty, but not so as to restrict the generality of the foregoing terms of this section, it is hereby declared that (notwithstanding anything in this Act) the exclusive legislative authority of the Parliament of Canada extends to all matters coming within the classes of subjects next hereinafter enumerated; that is to say:

1. The Public Debt and Property.
2. The Regulation of Trade and Commerce.
3. The Raising of Money by any mode or system of Taxation.
4. The Borrowing of Money on the Public Credit.
5. Postal Service.
6. The Census and Statistics.
7. Militia, Military and Naval Service, and Defence.
8. The Fxing of and Providing for the Salaries and Allowances of Civil and other Officers of the Government of Canada.
9. Beacons, Buoys, Lighthouses, and Sable Island.
10. Navigation and Shipping.
11. Quarantine and the Establishment and Maintenance of Marine Hospitals.
12. Sea coast and Inland Fisheries.
13. Ferries between a Province and any British or Foreign country or between two Provinces.
14. Currency and Coinage.
15. Banking, Incorporation of Banks, and the Issue of Paper Money.
16. Savings Banks.
17. Weights and Measures.
18. Bills of Exchange and Promissory Notes.

19. Interest.
20. Legal Tender.
21. Bankruptcy and Insolvency.
22. Patents of Invention and Discovery.
23. Copyrights.
24. Indians, and Lands Reserved for the Indians.
25. Naturalization and Aliens.
26. Marriage and Divorce.
27. The Criminal Law, except the Constitution of Courts of Criminal Jurisdiction, but including the Procedure in Criminal Matters.
28. The Establishment, Maintenance, and Management of Penitentiaries.
29. Such classes of subjects as are expressly excepted in the enumeration of the classes of subjects by this Act assigned exclusively to the Legislatures of the Provinces.

And any matter coming within any of the classes of subjects enumerated in this section shall not be deemed to come within the class of matters of a local or private nature comprised in the enumeration of the classes of subjects by this Act assigned exclusively to the Legislatures of the Provinces."

EXCLUSIVE POWERS OF PROVINCIAL LEGISLATURES

"92. In each Province the Legislature may exclusively make laws in relation to matters coming within the classes of subjects next hereinafter enumerated, that is to say:

1. The Amendment from time to time, notwithstanding anything in this Act, of the Constitution of the Province, except as regards the office of Lieutenant-Governor.
2. Direct Taxation within the Province in order to the raising of a Revenue for Provincial purposes.
3. The Borrowing of Money on the sole credit of the Province.
4. The Establishment and Tenure of Provincial Offices and the Appointment and Payment of Provincial Officers.
5. The Management and Sale of the Public Lands belonging to the Province and of the timber and wood thereon.
6. The Establishment, Maintenance, and Management of Public and Reformatory Prisons in and for the Province.
7. The Establishment, Maintenance and Management of Hospitals, Asylums, Charities, and Eleemosynary Institutions in and for the Province, other than Marine Hospitals.
8. Municipal Institutions in the Province.
9. Shop, Saloon, Tavern, Auctioneer, and other Licences in order to the raising of a Revenue for Provincial, local, or municipal purposes.
10. Local Works and Undertakings other than such as are of the following classes:
    (a) Lines of steam or other Ships, Railways, Canals, Telegraphs, and other works and undertakings connecting the Province with any other or others of the Provinces, or extending beyond the limits of the Province;

    (*b*) Lines of Steam Ships between the Province and any British or Foreign Country;

    (*c*) Such works as, although wholly situate within the Province, are before or after their execution declared by the Parliament of Canada to be for the general advantage of Canada or for the advantage of two or more of the Provinces.

11. The Incorporation of Companies with Provincial objects.
12. The Solemnization of Marriage in the Province.
13. Property and Civil Rights in the Province.
14. The Administration of Justice in the Province, including the Constitution, Maintenance, and Organization of Provincial Courts, both of Civil and of Criminal Jurisdiction, and including Procedure in Civil Matters in those Courts.
15. The Imposition of Punishment by fine, penalty, or imprisonment for enforcing any law of the Province made in relation to any matter coming within any of the classes of subjects enumerated in this section.
16. Generally all matters of a merely local or private nature in the Province."

The words "exclusive," "exclusively" are not employed to mean and they do not mean that the Imperial Parliament thereby divested itself of the power to legislate for Canada—that paramount power exists and the Imperial Parliament can legally exercise it. The words refer to the relative powers of Dominion and Provinces only.

[14]Substantially the language of Lord Selborne, Lord Chancellor, in The Queen v. Burah, (1878), 3 A. C. 889, at pp. 904, 905.

[15]The language of Sir Charles Moss, C. J. of Ontario, in Florence etc., v. Cobalt, etc., (1909), 18 Ont. Law Rep., 275, at p. 293. In the same case, I said at p. 279: "The prohibition 'Thou shalt not steal' has no legal validity upon the sovereign body." This decision roused the wrath of the late Professor Goldwin Smith, but no one now can doubt its correctness. It must not be supposed that such powers exist in a Provincial Legislature when the property affected by the legislation is without the Province. See the case in the Judicial Committee of the Privy Council, Royal Bank of Canada v. Rex, (1913), A. C. 283, reversing the Alberta Courts, (1912) 4 Alta. L. R. 249 (Trial) and 263 (Appeal).

In Ontario, when the constitutional validity of any enactment of the Dominion or Province is brought in question before a Court, the enactment cannot be declared invalid or *ultra vires* until notice has been given to the Attorney-General for Canada and the Attorney-General of Ontario, who are as of right entitled to be heard either in person or by counsel in any such case. Rev. Stat. Ont., (1914), C. 56, sec. 33.

[16]For example, the Dominion gave power to a Paper Controller concerning the supply of paper etc.; he made certain orders, and it was held that they were valid. Manitoba Free Press Co. Ltd., v. Fort Frances Pulp & Paper Co. Ltd., (1922) 22 Ont. W. N. 56, 277: "If the Dominion have regulative power over any class of subjects, it may exercise that power through any agency selected by itself. The power of the Dominion is not a delegated power and the

maxim *Delegatus non protest delegare* has no application;" Riddell, J., 22 Ont. W. N. at p. 37.

The Province of Ontario gave to certain Commissioners authority to make by-laws for the regulation of Taverns, &c.—as it was put by Hagarty, C. J., Q. B., "The Ontario legislature [assumed] to vest in the License Board the power of creating new offences and annexing penalties for their commission." Rex v. Hodge, (1881), 46 U. C., Q. B., 141 at p. 146. This legislation the Court of Appeal for Ontario held valid, S. C., (1882), 7 Ont. A. R., 246; and the decision was affirmed by the Judicial Committee of the Privy Council, Hodge v. The Queen, (1883), 9 A. C., 117.

Natural gas becoming less plentiful, the Province of Ontario in 1921 by the Act, 11 Geo. V, C. 17, (Ont.), gave the Minister of Mines the power to close and cut off the supply of natural gas to any corporation or individual, to cut off the supply to customers generally or to any customer or customers in any locality for such periods and for such times as he should deem proper etc., etc., and permitted any of these powers to be delegated to a Natural Gas Commissioner. This was held valid, Re Hill v. Glenwood N. Gas Co., *coram me*, April 5, 1923.

That the exercise of power within the jurisdiction is without limit is shown by such cases as Florence v. Cobalt etc., *ut suprâ*. In this last-named case it was held that the Province had the power to take away the land of A and give it to B without compensation. The whole doctrine of Eminent Domain has no importance in Canada. Certain rights on the River Kaministiqua were in 1897 and 1899 given to a named person by Acts in the Legislature of Ontario; these were taken away by an Act in 1902 and restored in 1904; no one ever questioned the validity of the legislation.

In Smith v. City of London, (1909), 20 Ont. L. Rep. 133, the right to stop litigation already begun and all future litigation on a stated subject was held to be in the Legislature of the Province. See also Delamatter v. Brown, (1908), 13 O. W. R., 58, at p. 63.

The Legislature not infrequently changes the provisions of wills. The first case to come to court in Ontario is referred to in re Goodhue: (1872), Grant's Chancery Reports, (Ontario), 366. The most recent instance of interference with the provisions of wills is referred to in re Hammond, (1921), 21 O. W. N. 100, 186; S. C. 51 Ont. L. R. 149. In 1916 the Legislature of Ontario established a Soldiers' Aid Commission to grant aid to returned soldiers, &c. 6 Geo. V, C. 3 (Ont.). This Act was amended in 1920 by 10, 11 Geo. V, C. 29, (Ont.), to aid and protect children of those who had served in the War; in 1917, by 7 Geo. V, C. 27, the Commission was given power to accept gifts and bequests and in 1919, it was by 9 Geo. V, C. 25, provided that if any will made before or after the Act made a bequest or devise for the benefit of any class of persons intended to be aided by the Commission or for any object within the powers of the Commission or for any purpose and it did not specify the particular person, society or institution to receive it, then the Commission was to be the beneficiary although "the executor or trustee . . . is directed to distribute such devise or bequest in the discretion of such executor or trustee." This was characterized by the Judge of first instance as "a retroactive Act doing violence to the wishes of the testator and confiscating the funds which he has set apart, taking them for the benefit of the Government of the Province which would otherwise have to provide the funds necessary for the carrying on of the work of the Commission." But neither Mr. Justice Middleton nor the Appellate Division (*quorum pars minima fui*) nor any Counsel thought of it being *ultra vires*.

It should however be stated that in the case of legislation in Ontario concerning any particular will, the proposed Act is submitted to two Justices of the Supreme Court, who, considering the circumstances alleged, advise the Legislature as to the fairness and justice of the measure. While without a favourable report the Legislature might pass the Bill, that is not likely to occur in practice.

The most striking legislation in this regard was passed in 1922 by the Legislature of the Province of Quebec. The facts may be stated at some length. In July, 1920, had occurred a shocking murder at Quebec of a young girl; in 1921, two men were arrested for the murder, tried and acquitted. "The Axe," a Montreal weekly, in its issue of October 27, 1922, published an article saying that the names of two Members of the Legislature were coupled with the crime and that it was freely and openly stated that the cause for the inaction of the authorities in clearing up the mystery was the fact of these two persons being Members. The Legislature was then in Session; the article was called to their attention, John D. Roberts, the editor of "The Axe" and President of the publishing company, was arrested and brought before the Legislative Assembly; he was questioned and refused to give the names of the two Members; the House declared him guilty "of having assailed its honour and its dignity by slandering two of its members in the most odious and atrocious manner;" a Bill was passed, *nem. con.*, by the House, concurred in by the Legislative Council and assented to by the Lieutenant Governor, December 29, 1922, to imprison Roberts for one year in the Common Gaol at Quebec; Roberts was taken to the Gaol the same day where he remained for more than three months. A writ of Habeas Corpus was refused by a Judge of the Superior Court at Quebec and by a Judge of the Supreme Court of Canada. An application was made to the Ministry at Ottawa to annul this Act; but before a decision was arrived at, Roberts admitted his error and he was released, April, 1923.

I know no better illustration of the different connotations of the word "constitutional" than is afforded by this case. Throughout Canada there was much comment upon the action of the Quebec Legislature in passing what was considered to be in effect *ex post facto* legislation to punish a past offence. Such a proceeding was argued to be unconstitutional in our British sense, i.e., a contention was made that it was contrary to the established principles of free government and to British usage in recent years.

The matter was discussed at a succeeding General Election in the Province at which the Government was sustained; consequently it must be considered that the people of that Province did not disapprove—and they are the ultimate authority. The Act, however, was of an extraordinary character and it is not likely to be followed frequently as a precedent.

CHAPTER II

THE EXECUTIVE AND LEGISLATURE

The B. N. A. Act by section 9 provides: "The Executive Government and authority of and over Canada is hereby declared to continue and be vested in the Queen;" and the provisions of the B. N. A. Act referring to the Queen extend also to Her heirs and successors, Kings and Queens of the United Kingdom.[1] Consequently, this Executive Government and authority is now vested in His Majesty King George V—in form.

No Sovereign has ever been in Canada.[2] But the Sovereign has a representative in the Governor-General who is appointed by the Home Administration; and all Acts, contracts, etc., are in the name of His Majesty.

In the Provinces, the Sovereign has a representative in the Lieutenant-Governor appointed by the Administration at Ottawa; but all Provincial Acts, contracts, etc., are also in the name of His Majesty. We shall see what is the substance under this form.

PARLIAMENT OF THE DOMINION

The Parliament of the Dominion meets at Ottawa[3] and is composed of two Houses, "an Upper House, styled the Senate, and the House of Commons."[4] The Senate at present consists of ninety-six members, who must be at least thirty years of age, and who are appointed for life by the Governor-General in the King's name,[5] twenty-four representing Ontario; twenty-four, Quebec; ten, Nova Scotia; ten, New Brunswick; four, Prince Edward Island; six, Manitoba; six, British Columbia; six, Saskatchewan, and six, Alberta.[6]

The Speaker of the Senate is appointed by the Governor-General, i.e., the Administration.[7]

Senators are in fact selected by the Administration for the time being; and for more than half a century have been of the political party of the appointing Administration.[8] The result is that when any political party is in power for any long time and is then defeated, the majorities in the two Houses of Parliament are for a time of opposite parties.[9]

Provision is made for vacating the seat of a Senator for failing to attend two consecutive Sessions of Parliament, bankruptcy, conviction of crime, foreign allegiance and failure of qualification in respect of property or residence.[10]

HOUSE OF COMMONS

Subject to one exception, representation in the House of Commons is on the population basis: Quebec has always sixty-five members; after each decennial census, each of the other Provinces has assigned to it such a number of members as will be in the same proportion to its population as ascertained by the census as the number sixty-five bears to the population of Quebec, so ascertained.[11]

The members are elected by voters on a franchise fixed by the Parliament of Canada. At the present time there are 235 Members.[12]

(1) Ontario	82	(6) Manitoba	15
(2) Quebec	65	(7) British Columbia	13
(3) Nova Scotia	16	(8) Alberta	12
(4) New Brunswick	11	(9) Saskatchewan	16
(5) Prince Edward Island	4	(10) Yukon Territory	1

THE LEGISLATURE OF THE PROVINCES

In two of the Provinces, Quebec and Nova Scotia, the Legislature consists of two Houses, the Legislative Council and Legislative Assembly;[13] in all the other Provinces, there is but one House, the Legislative Assembly.[14]

The members of the Legislative Assembly are elected on a franchise fixed by the Legislature of the Province.[15]

THE MINISTRY

The B. N. A. Act in the Preamble states that the uniting Provinces had "expressed their desire to be federally united —with a Constitution similar in principle to that of the United Kingdom." In reading the B. N. A: Act and all other documents, it must always be kept in mind that the Constitution of Canada and of its Provinces is similar in principle to that of the United Kingdom. Failing to bear this in mind will lead to the gravest errors in the interpretation of the Statutes, etc.; old forms are retained, but the whole spirit is revolutionized.

The underlying and cardinal principle of the Constitution of Canada, as of the Constitution of the United Kingdom, is Responsible Government—every executive officer is responsible for his every act to the representatives of the people elected to the House of Commons—and whatever may be the wording of any document, that principle must be borne in mind.

The B. N. A. Act provides that "there shall be a Council to aid and advise in the Government of Canada to be styled the Queen's Privy Council for Canada; and the persons who are to be members of that Council shall be from time to time chosen and summoned by the Governor-General and sworn in as Privy Councillors, and members thereof may be from time to time removed by the Governor-General."

This would indicate that the Governor-General had the duty of selecting and removing Privy Councillors, and that the Privy Councillors were the advisers of the Governor-General in the Government of Canada, the responsibility for which was cast upon him.

The fact is wholly different—the responsibility for the government of Canada rests upon a body of men not even

mentioned in the legislation—the "Cabinet" or "Ministry."
The Privy Council does exist and has as its members all the
present Ministry and the surviving members of past Minis-
tries; but it, as a whole, is *fainéant*—as a whole, it has no
duties and performs no functions. The duties and functions
assigned to the Privy Council in the B. N. A. Act are all
performed by the "Ministry" (the members of which, indeed,
are Privy Councillors). A Minister is generally sworn in as
a Privy Councillor on taking office, and remains a Privy
Councillor until his death: he takes no part in the government of the country after he retires from office unless and
until he becomes again a Minister. The political party in
the majority in the House of Commons selects a leader by
some process, formal or informal, and that leader becomes
Prime Minister; the Prime Minister selects the other
ministers so as to form a body of men who can obtain the
support and vote of a majority of the House of Commons.
While, so far as any written law goes, it is open to the
Governor-General to select anyone as Prime Minister, he
must in fact select the person whom the majority of the
House of Commons will follow, either the existing House of
Commons or a House obtained by a new General Election.[16]

So long as any Ministry can on a test vote [17] obtain a
majority in the House of Commons, it remains in power—so
soon as it fails it must resign, unless it can obtain a majority
on a new General Election.

Where a Ministry fails to obtain a majority at a General
Election, it must resign; and it is the recent practice to do so
with all convenient speed after the adverse result of the
Election is known and without waiting for an adverse vote
of the House of Commons.

While it is open to any Minister to resign at any time, yet
so long as the Ministry lasts, there can be no expressed
difference of opinion on any Government measure or
action—whatever brawls disturb the Council Chamber,

there must be unanimity in the position taken in public—the Ministry must be one. Whenever a Minister disagrees with his brethren in a matter of governmental action he should resign; he cannot avoid his constitutional responsibility for every governmental action or measure taken while he is a Minister.

The Ministers are responsible to the House of Commons; the Governor-General is not, nor are the Ministers responsible to him.[18]

All Ministers are "appointed by the Governor-General by commission under the Great Seal";[19] but never by the personal selection of the Governor-General; he takes and can take no active part in such selection—such a course would be unconstitutional in the Canadian sense of the word, it would certainly be resented and would destroy the usefulness of the offender.

"The Cabinet" is a term unknown to the Statutes as is the term "The Ministry"; but the Cabinet or Ministry is the actual governing body responsible for the government of Canada: and the acts directed by law to be done by the Governor-General, are in fact done by that body.

RELATIONS OF MINISTRY TO PARLIAMENT

The Ministry is responsible for the general course of legislation by Parliament; many bills are "Government Bills" and are brought into Parliament by a Minister. If a Government Bill should fail to obtain a majority, the Bill may be withdrawn, the Ministry not caring to risk their official existence on it—or it may be pressed to a vote. If on a muster of strength, a measure upon which the Ministry rests its fate, fails to obtain a majority, it shows that the Ministry no longer has the confidence of the House.

Measures which are not promoted by the Government are sometimes passed, having been introduced by private members; the Ministry, however, must in all cases take the responsibility of the Governor-General assenting thereto in the name of the Sovereign [20] and so permitting a "Bill" to become an "Act." [21]

Every Minister must have a seat in one or other of the Houses of Parliament;[22] and where a member of the House of Commons is made a Minister with a Portfolio and therefore with a salary, his seat is vacated and he must go back to constituents for re-election.[23]

MINISTRY IN THE PROVINCES

The position in the Provinces of the Ministry in reference to the Lieutenant-Governor and Legislature corresponds to that in the Dominion of the Ministry in reference to the Governor-General and Parliament.

RELATIONS OF CANADA WITH BRITAIN

To a non-Canadian there is nothing more puzzling and anomalous than the position of Canada in relation to the United Kingdom; and the utmost care is necessary in distinguishing form from substance, appearance from reality, the past from the present.

The Sovereign of the United Kingdom of Great Britain and Ireland is still and will doubtless continue to be Sovereign of Canada: but he does not in any way interfere with either its government or its legislation.

His representative is the Governor-General appointed by the Administration at Westminster, but always after conference with the Canadian Government. The King reigns but he does not rule; the Governor-General neither reigns nor rules. He brings with him Royal Instructions for his conduct in his office, but for all practical purposes he might be as well without them—his constitutional position is quite well known.[24]

It is in law within the power of the Imperial Parliament to legislate for all the British world, including Canada—

legislation concerning Canada would be undoubtedly valid in law, but that for which the Fathers of the Revolution fought, namely, that there should be no legislation without representation, is now thoroughly established in the British Commonwealth. Now for the Imperial Parliament to legislate for Canada without her previous request or subsequent assent, would be unconstitutional, and such a proceeding is unthinkable.[25]

The reservation of Canadian Statutes for the pleasure of the Sovereign is effete; it is now never done.[26]

So also the refusal to give the Royal consent.[27]

The provision in the B. N. A. Act that the Sovereign-in-Council may disallow any Canadian Statute within two years is equally effete.[28]

RELATIONS WITH THE UNITED STATES

For more than a century the boundary line between the United States and Canada was at some point or other in dispute; that has, however, now been settled more or less satisfactorily but finally.[29] Now the only questions are in essence commercial, the international Waterways and the Tariff—in all such matters Canada has full power to negotiate and does so.[30]

The question of the appointment of an Ambassador from Canada to the United States is still under consideration.[31]

RELATIONS WITH FOREIGN COUNTRIES

These are all of course commercial; Canada has a free hand in such matters.[32]

NOTES TO CHAPTER II

[1] B. N. A. Act, sec 2:

The style, United Kingdom of Great Britain and Ireland, will probably continue to be used notwithstanding any change past, present or to come in the relationships between Great Britain and Ireland. Such titles are conservatively retained: although the last vestige of English rule over territory in France disappeared on the conquest of Calais in Queen Mary's time in 1558, the Kings of England continued to be called Kings of France until

1801. King George III was "by the Grace of God of Great Britain, France and Ireland, King," in the Statutes of 1800 (see Statutes at Large, 14 Runnington, 18 Ruffhead, p. 537); but the next year, 1801, after the formation of the United Kingdom of Great Britain and Ireland, he was no longer called King of France—(see Stat. of United Kingdom, Tomlins' Ed. 1840, p. 1)—but "of the United Kingdom of Great Britain and Ireland."

²Albert Edward, Prince of Wales, afterwards King Edward VII, was in Canada in 1860 and the present King was also in Canada during his father's lifetime; the present Prince of Wales has also been in Canada; but no King or Queen has ever crossed the Atlantic when Sovereign.

³B. N. A. Act, sec. 16.

⁴B. N. A. Act, sec. 17.

⁵B. N. A. Act, sec. 24.

⁶By the B. N. A. Act, sec. 22, the Senate was to consist of 72 members; Canada was in relation to the constitution of the Senate to consist of three divisions, 1, Ontario, 2, Quebec, and 3, The Maritime Provinces (i.e., Nova Scotia and New Brunswick); and each division was to have 24 Senators, i.e., Ontario represented by 24 senators, Quebec represented by 24 senators, Nova Scotia represented by 12 senators, New Brunswick represented by 12 senators—72 in all.

When the Province of Manitoba was formed in 1870, it was given two members in the Senate until its population became 50,000 when it was to have three members until its population became 75,000 and then four, (1870), 33 Vict. C. 3., s. 3. (Dom.).

British Columbia came in in 1871 with three members. (Order in Council at Windsor, May 16, 1871, see Dominion Statutes for 1872, pp. lxxiv, sqq.) Prince Edward Island came in in 1873 with four members as provided by the B. N. A. Act, sec. 146; Alberta and Saskatchewan were formed in 1905 with four members each, (1905), 4, 5 Edw. VII, C. 3. sec. 4 (Dom.), 1905, 4, 5, Edw. VII, C. 42, sec. 4. (Dom.).

By the Act, (1915), 5, 6 Geo. V, C. 45. (Imp.) the Divisions of Canada in reference to the constitution of the Senate were made four—(1) Ontario (2) Quebec (3) Nova Scotia, New Brunswick and Prince Edward Island and (4) the Western Provinces—each represented by 24 Senators as in the Text mentioned.

The B. N. A. Act by sec. 26 provides "If at any time on the recommendation of the Governor-General the Queen thinks fit to direct that three or six members be added to the Senate, the Governor-General may by summons to three or six qualified persons (as the case may be) representing equally the three Divisions of Canada, add to the Senate accordingly."

This power was intended to be exercised only where an increase should be necessary to bring the Houses into accord "in the event of an actual collision of a serious and permanent character," "a difference of so serious and permanent a character that the government could not be carried on without such intervention:" it was not intended to be exercised simply to remedy the preponderance of Senators on the other side of politics from that of the majority of the House of Commons.

The exercise of this power has been asked for only once (in 1874), and the request was refused; it must be a very extraordinary juncture in which it can be asked for again.

[7] B. N. A. Act, sec. 34. The Speaker of the Senate is sometimes a member of the Cabinet. The Speaker of the House of Commons is elected by the House.

[8] I do not enter here into the vexed questions whether the intention of the framers of the B. N. A. Act, the "Fathers of Confederation", was that Senators should be selected irrespective of politics and whether in fact they were ever so selected.

[9] This was the case when the Conservative Party was defeated in 1896, having been in power since 1878; and also when the Reform Party was defeated in 1911 at the "Reciprocity Election", having been in power from 1896.

[10] B. N. A. Act, sec. 31—the age property and residence qualification is prescribed in sec. 23—he must be 30 years of age, a freeholder (or its equivalent in Quebec law) worth $4000 in the Province, and worth $4000 over and above his liabilities, and must reside in his Province.

[11] B. N. A. Act, sec. 51—the exception referred to is in the case of Prince Edward Island whose representation in the House of Commons would by the rule be reduced to three, but by virtue of the Act, (1915), 5, 6 Geo. V, C. 45 (Imp.) sec. 2, it has still four members as it has four Senators. This was the result of a protest by Prince Edward Island, acceded to by the rest of the Dominion. A section, 51A, was introduced into the B. N. A. Act, reading:—
"Notwithstanding anything contained in this Act, a Province shall always be entitled to a number of members in the House of Commons not less than the number of Senators representing such Province."

[12] "The Representation Act, 1914", 4, 5, Geo. V, C. 51. (Dom.), gives Prince Edward Island three members with the proviso that if the B. N. A. Act should be amended in accordance with a petition to be presented to His Majesty from Parliament the Province should have four. The amendment was made by the Act, (1915), 5, 6. Geo. V, C. 45, s. 2. (Imp.).

The number of members for each Province is automatically determined by the population and the B. N. A. Act and Amendments. The constituencies on readjustment are settled by a Committee of the House on which all political parties are represented: the report of the Committee is, of course, subject to change by the House. Of recent years, the action of Committee and House has been reasonably impartial and satisfactory: "Gerrymandering" was sometimes alleged in former times by political enemies of the party in power.

[13] Rev. Stat., Que., (1909), Art. 81; Rev. Stat., N. S., (1900), C. 2. In Nova Scotia, the Lower House is called the House of Assembly.

[14] Ontario had but one House from the beginning, 1867; British Columbia came into the Dominion, 1871, with one House; Alberta and Saskatchewan were formed, 1905, with one House; New Brunswick had originally two Houses, 1867; Prince Edward Island came in, 1873, with two and Manitoba was formed, 1867, with two. These three abolished the Legislative Council in 1891, 1873, and 1876 respectively.

The single House is except in Nova Scotia called the Legislative Assembly, R. S. O. (1914) C. 5, C. 1, s. 29 (d); R. S. B. C. (1911), C. 137; R. S. Alta. (1922), C. 3; R. S. Sask. (1920), C. 2.; R. S., N. B. (1903), C. 3; Acts P. E. I. (1913), C. 1, etc.; R. S. Man. (1913), C. 25 cf. 1913–14 C. 25, s. 96. In the Yukon Territory, there is a Council to aid the Commissioner who is the chief Executive officer and is appointed by the Ottawa Administration: the Council consists of three members, elected on a suffrage fixed by the Commissioner. See Note on the Territories, p. 49 *post*.

[15] Practically manhood franchise without distinction of sex.

[16] In a not very dissimilar way, the Electoral College may elect any qualified person President of the United States—but they must (in fact and in practice) elect the nominee of the political Party by whom the majority themselves were elected.

This kind of "camouflage" is not unlike the process for the election of a Bishop in the Church of England. When at the Reformation, the power of the Pope in the matter was put an end to, the Statute, (1533), 25 Henry VIII, C. 20, s. 4, provided that on a vacancy the King might grant to Dean and Chapter of the Cathedral a licence under the Great Seal—what is called a Congé d'Elire—to elect a Bishop "with a Letter Missive containing the name of the person which they shall elect and choose." The Governor-General has in fact no more choice than the Dean and Chapter.

[17] As distinguished from a "snap vote". in which by chance or misunderstanding, confidence in the Ministry is not understood to be in question or advantage is taken of an accidental absence of Government supporters and the "Government is caught napping."

Sometimes the Ministry makes it clear in advance that a measure introduced by a Minister is not one upon which they require their followers to vote with them—for example in Manitoba, April 27, 1923, the Wheat Board Bill, introduced in the Legislature by Premier John Bracken, providing for Manitoba's participation in the establishment of a western compulsory wheat board, was defeated in the Legislature when the measure was up for second reading. The vote was 24 to 21. Although the measure was brought before the House by a member of the Cabinet, its rejection did not involve the defeat of the Government, as the Prime Minister made it clear that the members of his party were not bound to vote for or against the measure.

[18] The Cabinet at Washington is the Cabinet of the President responsible to him, not to the House of Representatives or the Senate. They carry out his policy and he is the final judge of what should be done; the reverse is the case in Ottawa as it is in London. Of course the American system is the former English system before Responsible Government.

[19] See, e.g., R. S. Can., (1906), C. 48, s. 3. "There shall be a department which shall be called the Department of Customs, over which the Ministry of Customs for the time being appointed by the Governor General under the Great Seal shall preside."

[20] B. N. A. Act, sec. 15. The assent of the Sovereign is necessary to the validity of an Act of Parliament. This assent is now a mere empty for-

mality: no sovereign has in England refused the Royal assent since William III refused his consent to the Bill for Triennial Parliaments in 1692; and no Governor-General has refused the Royal Assent when advised by the Ministers to give it. The Governor-General is the only man in Canada who has no right to an opinion in party or political matters; he is "merely the motionless representative of the monarchical principle." See Porrett's Unreformed House of Commons, Vol. 1, p. 407.

So in a Province the Lieutenant-Governor is the only man who has no right to an opinion on any political matter. Very shortly after these Lectures were delivered, a deadlock was reported to have taken place in the Government in Manitoba—Sir James Aikins, the Lieutenant-Governor, being asked about it said:—"I do not act except on the advice of the First Minister or Acting Premier, and I cannot speak except through them on matters relating to the Administration—this is well known."

[21] At the present time there are nineteen in the Cabinet or Ministry, of whom sixteen have Departments and three are "Ministers without Portfolio," all but one in the House of Commons. It has, however, been the custom to have not less than two Cabinet Ministers in the Senate, sometimes three.

[22] There is no statutory or other written prohibition against a non-member being a Minister. It is part of the unwritten constitution, and for a Minister to violate the rule would be unconstitutional in our sense. Instances have been known of a Minister being for a short time without a seat in either House; but that must be overcome or the Minister must resign.

[23] See R. S. C., (1906), C. 10, ss. 10, 11, 12, 13. This is an old rule in England first made certain and definite in 1705 by the Act, 4, 5 Anne, C. 20. The legal provisions are that by a Member of the House of Commons accepting an office of emolument under the Crown, his seat becomes vacant R. S. C. (1904), C. 10, s. 10 (a); but if that office be any of the portfolios he is not disqualified "if he is elected while he holds such office," do. do. s. 12. A provision is made that the acceptance of a portfolio within a month of a previous resignation of a portfolio shall not vacate the seat: do. do. s. 13. It was a similar provision, passed *alio intuitu*, which enabled a defeated Government which had resigned to resume the reins of power without going to the people—the celebrated "Double Shuffle" in 1858. See Lewis, Life of George Brown, Makers of Canada Series, Toronto, 1906, chap. X, pp. 99 sqq: Pope's Memoirs of Sir John A. Macdonald, Ottawa, n. d. Vol. 1, pp. 198–204. Particulars of this case are given in note 7 to Chapter III, p. 43, *post*.

[24] There is possibly one exception to this: that is in the matter of persons convicted of crime. Until 1878 the old form of Royal Instructions was adhered to by which the Governor-General was understood to consult the Ministry in all cases of application for clemency, etc., but was at liberty to disregard their advice. The Canadian Minister of Justice, Hon. Edward Blake, took up the matter with the Home Authorities with the result that when in 1878, the Queen's son-in-law, the Marquis of Lorne, was appointed Governor-General, the Instructions were varied. The Imperial authorities

agreed to the proposition that in all cases of a merely Canadian nature, the advice of the Canadian Ministers should prevail.

The result is that the Governor-General is in such matters, as in all others, bound to follow the advice of the Ministry. One instance, indeed, occurred in the time of the Earl of Aberdeen when under very peculiar circumstances, the Ministry allowed the Governor-General to commute a capital sentence without advising it; nevertheless, the Ministry were held constitutionally responsible for the act.

The clause in the Royal Instructions relating to pardons, etc., is worth transcribing in full, as showing the form of such papers:

"V. And we do further authorize and empower Our said Governor-General, as he shall see occasion, in Our name and on Our behalf, when any crime or offence against the Laws of Our said Dominion has been committed for which the offender may be tried therein, to grant a pardon to any accomplice, in such crime or offence, who shall give such information as shall lead to the conviction of the principal offender, or of any one of such offenders if more than one; and further, to grant to any offender convicted of any such crime or offence in any Court, or before any Judge, or Magistrate, within Our said Dominion, a pardon, either free or subject to lawful conditions, or any respite of the execution of the sentence of any such offender, for such period as to Our said Governor-General may seem fit and to remit any fines, penalties or forfeitures which may become due and payable to Us. Provided always that Our said Governor-General shall not in any case, except where the offence has been of a political nature, make it a condition of any pardon or remission of sentence that the offender shall be banished from or shall absent himself from Our said Dominion. And we do hereby direct and enjoin that Our said Governor-General shall not pardon or reprieve any such offender without first receiving in capital cases the advice of the Privy Council for Our said Dominion, and in other cases the advice of one, at least, of his Ministers: and in any case in which such pardon or reprieve might directly affect the interests of Our Empire, or of any country or place beyond the jurisdiction of the Government of Our said Dominion, Our said Governor-General shall, before deciding as to either pardon or reprieve, take those interests specially into his own personal consideration in conjunction with such advice as aforesaid."

It cannot be said with absolute accuracy that the Governor-General is wholly without power in the matter.

[25]Imperial Statutes are undoubtedly legally binding in Canada—cf. B. N A. Act sec. 129—and "no Court of law would venture to question the right of (the Imperial) Parliament to legislate in any case or upon any question or . . . assert that any Act of the Imperial Parliament was *ultra vires.*" Todd, Parliamentary Government in the Colonies, 2nd Edit. London, p. 245.

Although the power still exists in law in the Imperial Parliament to legislate for Canada—see Chapter I, note 15 *supra*—it would be unconstitutional to do so in the case of matters purely Canadian. Statutes of the Imperial Parliament in their supposed application must be read in the light of a statutory provision in 1865 when Canada was still a "Colony"; the Act (1865) 28, 29 Vict. C. 63 (Imp.) by Sec. 1 provides that in construing supposed conflicting Imperial and Colonial legislation, "An Act of Parliament or any provision thereof shall be said to extend to any Colony when it is made applicable to such Colony by express words or necessary implication."

Moreover in some cases where otherwise the self-governing Dominions would be affected, the Act contains a clause such as that in the Seal Fisheries Act, (North Pacific) (1912) 2, 3, Geo. V, C. 10, s. 5 (Imp.): "Provided that those provisions shall not be extended to a self-governing dominion except with the consent of the Governor-General in Council or Governor in Council of the Dominion."

The Imperial War Cabinet, formed in 1917, passed a resolution: "they deem it their duty . . . to place on record their views that any such readjustment [of the constitutional relations of the component parts of the Empire] while thoroughly preserving all existing powers of self-government and complete control of domestic affairs should be based upon a full recognition of the Dominions as autonomous nations of an Imperial Commonwealth." In May, 1921, Sir Robert Borden, the Prime Minister of Canada, declared that the relations between the constituent parts of the Empire must be based upon a conception of complete freedom and equality in national status. In 1919, Lord Milner, an Imperial statesman, said "The only possibility of a continuance of the British Empire is on a basis of absolute out-and-out equal partnership between the United Kingdom and the Dominions."

[26] When Britain actually ruled Canada, it was the custom to direct the Governor-General (in the Royal Instructions) to reserve for the Sovereign's pleasure certain classes of Bills—this was put an end to in 1878 and since that time there has not even been any semblance of authority for such a course. Before Confederation the practice was very common: but since that event there has been no instance of the kind.

In the Provinces before 1882, certain Bills passed by the Legislature were on the advice of the Provincial Ministry reserved by the Lieutenant-Governor for the Governor-General's assent. The Ottawa administration took the matter into consideration and declaring that the relations of the Lieutenant-Governor with his responsible advisers were the same as those of the Governor-General with his, asserted that "the Lieutenant-Governor is not warranted in reserving any measure for the assent of the Governor-General on the advice of his Ministers—he should do so in his capacity of a Dominion officer only and on instructions from the Governor-General." It is pointed out that the principles of constitutional government require that the Ministry must of necessity have the confidence of the majority in the popular House, and therefore they generally control or rather direct current legislation—if they allow a Bill to pass, they cannot advise its rejection by the Sovereign.

The Lieutenant-Governors were accordingly so instructed and the objectionable practice has completely ceased.

[27] Refusing the Royal assent to a Bill is technically different from reserving it for the Sovereign's pleasure—in times before Responsible Government,

when the Governor still actually governed, if legislation was passed of which he disapproved, he had the power—and could constitutionally use it—to refuse the Royal Assent without communicating with England. As we have seen, the Royal Assent has in England never been withheld since 1692 in the time of King William III, and it has never been refused in the Dominion of Canada.

Even should the Royal Instructions direct the Governor to refuse the Royal Assent, still if he did give such Assent, the Act was not invalid, (1865) 28, 29 Vict., C. 63, s. 4 (Imp.): this had already been decided by the Supreme Court of New Brunswick, Reg. v. J. Kerr, (1838), 2 N. B. Rep. (Berthon) 367, 558. Cf. Bk. of Australasia v. Noris, (1857), 16 Q. B., 717.

[28] This power was exercised only once and then at the instance of the Canadian Ministry. In 1873, the Houses of Parliament of Canada passed a Bill to provide for the examination of witnesses on oath by Committees of either of the Houses: Lord Dufferin gave the Royal Assent; the Minister of Justice, Sir John A. Macdonald (who was also Prime Minister) in a memorandum to the Governor-General expressed grave doubts as to the measure being *intra vires* the Canadian Parliament. The matter was submitted to the Law Officers of the Crown in London and they gave their opinion that the Bill was *ultra vires;* it consequently was disallowed. The Canadian Ministry did not and could not escape responsibility for the memorandum—it was charged that the proceedings were a design to prevent an investigation into certain transactions of the Ministry.

The course taken in this instance would not now be followed—the validity of the Statute would be referred to the Supreme Court of Canada for decision under the Dominion Act, R. S. C., (1906), C. 139, Sec. 60, which reads:

"Important questions of law or fact touching—(a) the interpretation of the British North America Acts, 1867 to 1886; or

(b) the constitutionality of or interpretation of any Dominion or provincial legislation; or

(c) the appellate jurisdiction as to educational matters, by The British North America Act, 1867, or by any other Act or law vested in the Governor in Council; or

(d) the powers of the Parliament of Canada, or of the legislatures of the provinces, or of the respective governments thereof, whether or not the particular power in question has been or is proposed to be executed; or

(e) any other matter, whether or not in the opinion of the court *e jusdem generis* with the foregoing enumerations, with reference to which the Governor in Council sees fit to submit any such question;

may be referred by the Governor in Council to the Supreme Court for hearing and consideration; and any question touching any of the matter aforesaid, so referred by the Governor in Council, shall be conclusively deemed to be an important question."

It will be observed that Provincial Legislation may also be thus referred. In certain of the Provinces, the Provincial authorities have the power of referring the validity of their Provincial legislation to the Courts.

For example in Ontario, the R. S. Ont., (1914), C. 85, ss. 2, 3 and 4, read as follows:

2. The Lieutenant-Governor in Council may refer to a Divisional Court or to a Judge of the Supreme Court for hearing and consideration any matter which he thinks fit and the Court shall thereupon hear and consider the same.

3. The Court shall certify to the Lieutenant-Governor in Council its opinion on the matter referred, accompanied by a statement of the reasons therefor; and any Judge who differs from the opinion may in like manner certify his opinion and his reasons.

4. Where the matter relates to the constitutional validity of any Act of this Legislature, or of some provision thereof, the Attorney-General for Canada shall be notified of the hearing in order that he may be heard if he sees fit."

While the Acts refer to "constitutionality," etc., it must be remembered that the written constitution only is meant—the Courts cannot determine whether an act is "constitutional" in any other sense.

[29]Foolish talk of readjusting the "North East" boundary between Maine and New Brunswick, and the boundary of Alaska will crop up now and then. It is nothing but irresponsible talk of unofficial but officious persons—the boundary is settled and no responsible person will make any serious proposal to unsettle it.

[30]Before 1871, while British negotiators sometimes availed themselves of Canadian advisers—as e.g. in the Elgin-Marcy Treaty of Reciprocity in 1854—still Canadians did not appear officially. In 1871, the Canadian Prime Minister, Sir John A. Macdonald, was one of the British Commissioners in the Treaty of Washington; and that Treaty by Art. 33 provided that certain clauses affecting Canada should come into effect only on legislation by Canada. In 1874, Hon. George Brown was at the instance of the Canadian Government appointed to act with the British Ambassador at Washington to negotiate for a Reciprocity Treaty of Commerce between the United States and Canada. In 1887, Sir Charles Tupper was a Plenipotentiary in respect of the Atlantic Fisheries negotiation; in 1892, his son, Sir Charles Hibbert Tupper, assisted in the Bering Sea Treaty; in 1898, by direct negotiation between the Governments of the United States and Canada, a Joint High Commission was appointed to negotiate as to certain matters affecting Canadian interests. On this Commission were three Canadians, Sir Wilfrid Laurier, Sir Richard Cartwright and Sir Louis Davies. In 1903, the Alaskan Boundary Treaty was in fact negotiated by Canadians though the British Ambassador acted as Plenipotentiary. In 1909, the Waterways Treaty was negotiated by Sir George Gibbons, a Canadian, under the direct supervision of Sir Wilfrid Laurier, the Canadian Prime Minister. So the Reciprocity negotiations of 1910 and 1911 were conducted by Canadian Ministers; and many attempts were made by Canadian Ministers theretofore to bring about Reciprocity. See further Lecture IV, note 28, pp. 68, 69, post.

[31]In 1882, 1889 and 1892, the matter of direct diplomatic representation

at Washington was discussed in the Canadian Parliament; in 1918, it was found necessary to establish a Canadian War Minister at Washington—in fact if not in form, a diplomatic mission; in 1920, after discussion with the British Government, it was agreed that His Majesty should on the advice of the Canadian Ministry "appoint a Minister Plenipotentiary who will have charge of Canadian affairs and will at all times be the ordinary channel of communication with the United States Government in matters of purely Canadian concern acting upon instructions from and reporting directly to the Canadian Government. In the absence of the Ambassador, the Canadian Minister will take charge of the whole Embassy and of the representation of Imperial as well as of Canadian interests." (May 10, 1920.) See Chapter IV, note 28, pp. 68, 69, *post*.

[22] I do not say "*other* Foreign Countries." We do not look upon the United States as really a "foreign" country.

In 1878, Sir A. T. Galt conducted negotiations with Spain and France but in form through the British Ambassador; in 1884, Sir Charles Tupper negotiated with Spain; in 1892–93 Sir Charles Tupper procured a Commercial Treaty with France.

The most interesting of the complications arising from Canadian Tariff legislation was in 1896–7; Canada proposed to give to British goods a preference by reducing the customs dues below those of goods of other origin. Germany and Belgium protested; they had treaties with Britain entitling them to as favorable a tariff as any other country in Britain and her Dependencies. Canada was,—and, for that matter, is,—in the theory of international law, a Dependency of Britain; Germany and Belgium were technically right, and their right was acknowledged by Canada. But at the meeting of the Colonial Conference in 1897, Sir Wilfrid Laurier, our Prime Minister, insisted that the obnoxious treaties should be denounced, and the "British Preference" became effective. To complete the story, Belgium submitted; Germany placed a surtax on Canadian goods, Canada promptly retaliated and Germany "came down."

See Chapter IV and Notes.

CHAPTER III

THE ELECTED LEGISLATIVE HOUSES

The judgment of the people must be taken from time to time by a General Election at which representatives are elected for the whole Dominion or Province: a vacancy in the popular House caused by death, resignation or acceptance of an office of emolument under the Crown[1] is filled at an election for the particular constituency generally called a By-election.

In the Dominion, the B. N. A. Act, by section 50, provides that "every House of Commons shall continue for five years from the day of the return of the writs for choosing the House (subject to be sooner dissolved by the Governor-General) and no longer"— consequently there must be a General Election at least as frequently as every five years.[2]

In the Provinces, the Act by section 85, provides that the Legislative Assembly is to continue for four years (subject to being sooner dissolved by the Lieutenant-Governor) and no longer—consequently there must be a Provincial General Election at least as frequently as every four years.[3]

In fact, the General Elections have been more frequent— in the Dominion, the House of Commons has had an average life of a little over four years; in the Province of Ontario (which is taken as an example) the average life of the Legislative Assembly had been a little under four years.[4]

The superior limit or maximum term being fixed, there is no inferior limit or minimum—a General Election may be had at any time.

MANNER OF CALLING A GENERAL ELECTION

The Governor-General has the power to dissolve the House of Commons at any time, but in such matters as in all others he must have or obtain a Ministry to take the responsibility of his act.

In all but very extraordinary cases, he acts upon the advice of the existing Ministry, but it is conceivable that a state of facts might arise in which he might constitutionally decline to follow their advice—he must, however, even in such a case find a Ministry to justify his act.

The most usual occasion for holding a General Election is when the existing Ministry considers for any reason that the opinion of the electorate should be taken either on the general policy of the Ministry or on some measure taken or proposed to be taken— sometimes, indeed, no reason can be seen except that the Ministers think the time favorable for their Party.[5]

Sometimes a Ministry is defeated in a House of Commons, thus showing lack of confidence of the House in it. The Ministry may resign or it may advise a General Election hoping to receive a favorable vote from the electorate. This is one of the few cases in which the Governor-General must exercise his judgment—he may accede to the request and then an Election is held, or he may refuse. If he does refuse, the Ministry must resign, the Governor-General must call upon a Leader of the dominant party to form a Ministry and relieve him of the responsibility for the refusal. Should the new Ministry be dissatisfied with the existing House, it may in its turn ask for a dissolution; and unless the Governor-General is prepared to take back the former Ministry and be guided by its advice, the request must be granted.[6] The actions of the Governor-General in granting or refusing a General Election are based on well established constitutional rules. He must avoid becoming a party man, he must not engage in party politics or political intrigue, he must hold the scales even in respect of all political parties, he must be guided by a fair and candid consideration of the welfare of the people at large, he must not grant a dissolution simply to enable a political party to continue in office when there is no real and important question at issue between the parties.[7]

However, the Governor-General has the right to be satisfied that the Ministers are men of personal integrity and honor whom he can trust: if and when the contrary is proved, he has not only the right but also the duty to dismiss them.[8] When he does so, he takes the chance of the House approving his conduct in so doing; and if a dissolution is granted, he takes the chance of the new House approving.

Not only is the Governor-General to the extent and in the manner just mentioned responsible to the people, but he is also responsible to the Imperial Administration. In theory an appeal may be made by a dissatisfied Ministry to the Imperial Secretary of State—this has never been done in the Dominion, and it is hard to conceive a state of facts in which it would be necessary or proper.[9]

While in the past, the King of Great Britain and Ireland occasionally dismissed his Ministers,[10] the time of the King's direct rule is gone. So, too, while it has been said with truth that the powers of the Governor-General in Canada are greater in some respects than those of the King in England, it is also true that the time of the Governor-General's direct rule in Canada is now no more.

IN THE PROVINCES

In the Provinces, the right and duties of the Lieutenant-Governor in respect of dissolution, etc., are the same as those of the Governor-General in the Dominion.[11]

The Lieutenant-Governor is responsible not only to the people (only, however, in the sense already noted in speaking of the Governor-General) but also to the Governor-

General-in-Council.[12] The B. N. A. Act provides that a Lieutentant-Governor shall not be removable within five years from his appointment except for cause assigned, communicated in writing to him and to the two Houses of Parliament.[13] The term of Lieutenant-Governors has not in general been interfered with; but there is no vested right to the full term, and the Governor-General-in-Council has complete control in law over it; [14] and, indeed, one case has occurred of removal under the provisions of the B. N. A. Act for what was considered improper conduct in respect of dissolving the Legislative Assembly.[15]

LEGISLATION IN DOMINION

The only provision in the B. N. A. Act as to the House in which legislation is to originate is in section 53: "Bills for appropriating any Part of the Public Revenue or for imposing any Tax or Impost shall originate in the House of Commons." [16]

The next section provides that "it shall not be lawful for the House of Commons to adopt or pass any Vote Resolution Address or Bill for the appropriation of any Part of the Public Revenue or of any Tax or Impost to any purpose that has not been first recommended to that House by Message of the Governor-General in the Session. . . ."

The act of the Governor-General in signing such a Message is purely formal and involves no judgment on his part as to the merits or propriety of the expenditure, etc., therein proposed: all such Messages are sent to the House through a Minister,[17] and are prepared by a Minister for the Governor-General's signature.

All other Bills may originate in either House; before being presented to the Governor-General, a Bill must pass both Houses.[18]

When a Bill has passed both Houses, it is by a Minister presented to the Governor-General for the assent of the

Sovereign and "he shall declare according to his discretion but subject to the provisions of this Act and to Her Majesty's instructions either (1) that he assents thereto in the Queen's name or (2) that he withholds the Queen's assent or (3) that he reserves the Bill for the signification of the Queen's pleasure."

This is substantially the same as the provision in the former Acts concerning Canada from the beginning: it keeps up the elaborate pretence that, as once was the case, Canada is still governed from England and that all her legislation must be satisfactory to the authorities at Westminster. In fact, the Governor-General acts on the advice of the Canadian Ministry and gives the Royal Assent accordingly—constitutionally, when a Bill has passed both Houses of Parliament (which can happen only by the consent or acquiescence of the Ministry), it must receive the Royal Assent, except in extraordinary circumstances.[19] Such assent has never been refused in the Dominion of Canada. Very few Bills have been reserved for the Royal pleasure and none since 1878 [20]—the practice is effete.

Even if the Royal Assent be given, there remains the legal power of disallowance by the Imperial Government within two years—this power has been exercised only once in Canadian legislation, and that practically at the instance of the Dominion Ministry.[21] The practice is that if an Act or any part of it seems objectionable, communications are had between the Imperial and Canadian Governments; and if the latter is satisfied of the validity of the objection, legislation is introduced in the following Session of the Canadian Parliament, to rectify the evil.

LEGISLATION IN THE PROVINCES

The B. N. A. Act by section 90 is considered to direct that Bills of the kind required in the Dominion to originate in the House of Commons shall in the Provinces originate in the Assembly.[22] This is, of course, superfluous where the Legislature is unicameral, and is of application only in Nova Scotia and Quebec.

In all the Provinces, all such Bills must have been first recommended by Message from the Lieutenant-Governor during the Session: and the same rules apply to such Bills in the Provinces as in the Dominion.

The power of the Legislative Council in bicameral Legislatures corresponds to that of the Senate in the Dominion Parliament.

In law, the Lieutenant-Governor has the same power in the Province as the Governor-General in the Dominion in respect of giving or refusing the Royal Assent and in reserving a Bill—if a Bill is reserved, it is reserved for the pleasure of the Governor-General. The control of the Crown over Provincial legislation is not exercised by the authorities in England; but solely by the Governor-General acting under the advice of Ministers responsible to the Dominion House of Commons.[23]

The reserving of Bills for the pleasure of the Governor-General is now practically effete:[24] there is generally no need for such a course, for the Governor-General-in-Council has the power of disallowing any Provincial Act within one year.

In such disallowance (as we have seen) the Governor-General acts on the advice of his Ministry; the Ministry is of course responsible to the House of Commons of Canada.

For some time after Confederation, the disallowance of Provincial measures by the Governor-General was rather common and the practice cannot be said to have been uniform—the rule now is that (speaking generally) the power of disallowance will not be exercised except in cases where the legislation is *ultra vires* or is considered injurious to the interests of Canada generally.[25]

CONFLICT OF LEGISLATIVE AUTHORITY

From what has been said, it is manifest that the Dominion has, in law, full control over Provincial legislation for a year; and, therefore, it might be inferred that Provincial legislation allowed to become law could never be found to trench upon the field of the Dominion. But sometimes Acts which do not seem to the Dominion Ministry to be objectionable, even when petitioned against by parties interested [26], and are consequently not disallowed, are afterwards found objectionable; sometimes, too, the full effect of a statute has not appeared until after the lapse of time. Any litigant may set up the invalidity of a statute, Dominion or Provincial— and the matter may be of such importance that the Dominion or Provincial authorities or both may intervene. When the validity of a statute is brought in question, the Court must decide according to the strict law—nothing is of consequence but the legal power. The B. N. A. Act is then interpreted in the same way and on the same principles as the Constitution of the United States is interpreted in American Courts.[27]

NOTES TO CHAPTER III

[1] In England a member of the House of Commons cannot resign his seat: one desiring to retire "applies for the Chiltern Hundreds"—i.e., he asks the Government to be, and as a matter of course, he is, appointed Steward of the Chiltern Hundreds, an office of purely nominal value under the Crown; and thereupon his seat becomes legally vacant. Sometimes, the Stewardship of the Manors of East Hendred, Northstead or Hempholme is selected instead.

In Canada, the Statute, R. S. C., (1906), C. 11, ss. 5, 6, provides for a member resigning his seat (a) by giving in his place in the House notice of his intention to resign, in which case as soon as the Clerk enters the notice on the Journal of the House, the Speaker directs the issue of a Writ for an election, or,

(b) by addressing and having delivered to the Speaker, a declaration of his intention to resign, signed and sealed before two witnesses. If the House is not in Session, and there is no Speaker or if the Speaker is absent from Canada or if the member be himself the Speaker, the declaration is delivered to any two members of the House and they direct the Writ to issue.

In the Province of Ontario, a member elected to the Legislative Assembly may resign before the Assembly meets by addressing and causing to be delivered to any two members of the Assembly a declaration signed before two witnesses: these two members then direct a Writ to issue for a new election for that constituency.

A member may resign his seat by giving in his place in the Assembly, notice of his intention to resign or by addressing and causing to be delivered to the Speaker, a declaration that he resigns his seat, signed before two witnesses.

If the Assembly is not in Session or the Speaker is absent from the Province or if the member is Speaker, the same practice is followed as in the Dominion except that the declaration need not be under seal. R. S. O., (1914), C. 11, ss. 23, 24, 25.

In neither the Dominion nor Province is a member allowed to resign his seat if his election is controverted or until the time has expired for filing a petition against it. R. S. C., (1906), C. 11, s. 8; R. S. O., (1914), C. 11, s. 26 (2).

If in ignorance of the fact that a member's election is petitioned against, the Speaker directs a Writ to issue for a new election, as soon as the fact comes to his knowledge, the Speaker issues a Warrant of Supersedeas, recalling the improper Writ of Election.

²We have seen that in one instance during the War the life of the House of Commons was (in 1916) extended for an additional year. See note 7 to Chapter 1, pp. 9, 10, ante.

NO.	BEGAN	PRIME MINISTER	PARTY	REMARKS
1	1867	Sir John A. Macdonald	Conservative	
2	1873	Sir John A. Macdonald ⎱	Conservative	
		Alexander Mackenzie ⎰	Reform	⎰ Pacific Scandal
3	1874	Alexander Mackenzie	Reform	⎱ Election
4	1878	Alexander Mackenzie ⎱	Reform	⎰ National Policy
		Sir John A. Macdonald ⎰	Conservative	⎱ Election
5	1883	Sir John A. Macdonald	Conservative	
6	1887	Sir John A. Macdonald	Conservative	
7	1891	Sir John A. Macdonald	Conservative	
8	1897	(Sir) Wilfrid Laurier	Reform	Manitoba School
9	1901	Sir Wilfrid Laurier	Reform	question
10	1905	Sir Wilfrid Laurier	Reform	
11	1909	Sir Wilfrid Laurier	Reform	
12	1911	(Sir) Robert Borden	Conservative	Reciprocity
13	1918	Sir Robert Borden ⎱	Conservative	Election
		Arthur Meighen ⎰	Conservative	
14	1922	W. L. Mackenzie King	Reform	

[3]We have seen that the Legislative Assembly of the Province of Ontario during the War extended its own life. See note 9 to Chapter I, p. 10, *ante*.

[4]From 1867 till 1921, 55 years, there were thirteen Parliaments of Canada, an average of four years and about a quarter.

In the Province of Ontario from 1867 to 1923, 56 years, there have been 15 Legislatures, an average of three years and about nine months.

NO.	BEGAN	PRIME MINISTER	PARTY	REMARKS
1	1867	John Sandfield Macdonald	Conservative	
2	1871	John Sandfield Macdonald	Conservative	Macdonald defeated in House
		Edward Blake	Reform	by desertion of
		(Sir) Oliver Mowat	Reform	members
3	1875	Sir Oliver Mowat	Reform	
4	1880	Sir Oliver Mowat	Reform	
5	1884	Sir Oliver Mowat	Reform	
6	1887	Sir Oliver Mowat	Reform	
7	1891	Sir Oliver Mowat	Reform	
8	1895	Sir Oliver Mowat ⎱ Arthur S. Hardy ⎰	Reform	
9	1898	Arthur S. Hardy ⎱ Geo. W. Ross ⎰	Reform	
10	1903	Sir Geo. W. Ross	Reform	
11	1905	(Sir) James P. Whitney	Conservative	
12	1909	Sir James P. Whitney	Conservative	
13	1912	Sir James P. Whitney ⎱ (Sir) William H. Hearst ⎰		
14	1915	Sir William H. Hearst	Conservative	
15	1920	Ernest C. Drury	Farmers' Pty	
16	1923	G. Howard Ferguson	Conservative	

[5]E.g., in 1911, Sir Wilfrid Laurier was desirous of receiving a mandate from the electorate to carry into effect the Reciprocity Treaty with the United States which had been negotiated and carried through Congress: although the 11th Parliament had nearly three years yet to run, and he had a majority in the House of Commons, he advised an appeal to the people. He was unsuccessful: the electorate proved adverse and Sir Wilfrid resigned.

[6]On the Election, in 1873, for the 2nd House of Commons of Canada, the Conservative party led by Sir John A. Macdonald was found to have a majority, and accordingly his Ministry continued in power. But in the first Session, the House was about to pass a vote of non-confidence in the Ministry, and Sir John, without awaiting the vote, resigned. Alexander Mackenzie who had become leader of the Reform Party on the defeat in his

constituency of George Brown, was sent for and charged with the formation of a Ministry. He asked for a General Election: Lord Dufferin, the Governor-General assented: at the ensuing election in January, 1874, the "Pacific Scandal Election", the Reform Party had a considerable majority, and Mackenzie was confirmed in his position.

The next General Election was in September, 1878—this was the "National Policy Election" in which the opponents of the Government called for "a judicious arrangement of the tariff for the benefit of the agricultural, mining, manufacturing and other interests"—a Protective Tariff, in short. The Conservatives had a majority, and after an adverse vote in October, 1875, Mackenzie resigned. Sir John A. Macdonald was called on to form a Ministry, which he did; being satisfied with the existing House of Commons, he did not ask for a new election.

Macdonald remained Prime Minister until his death in June, 1891, having successfully appealed to the electorate in the 5th, 6th and 7th General Elections as well as the 1st, 2nd and 4th. He was succeeded by (Sir) John J. C. Abbott who resigned in 1892, Sir John S. D. Thompson who died in 1894, Sir Mackenzie Bowell who resigned in 1896, and Sir Charles Tupper, all Conservatives. The 7th Parliament expired by lapse of time and at the ensuing General Election (Manitoba School Question Election) in 1896, the Reform Party obtained a majority in the House: Sir Charles Tupper resigned without meeting the House and (Sir) Wilfrid Laurier, a Reformer, succeeded as Prime Minister. He was successful in the General Elections of 1901, 1905 and 1909, but going to the country in 1911 on the Reciprocity Treaty, he was defeated. He resigned without meeting the House and (Sir) Robert Laird Borden became Prime Minister. The term of the 12th Parliament being extended by Imperial legislation, there was no General Election till 1917—at this election, the Conservatives (combined with certain Reformers) had a majority, and Sir Robert Borden remained Prime Minister. He resigned during the life of the House and was succeeded by Arthur Meighen, who went down to defeat in the General Election of 1921. William Lyon Mackenzie King, the Leader of the Reform Party, became Prime Minister and still (May, 1923) fills that position.

In the Province of Ontario, the first Prime Minister, John Sandfield Macdonald, was defeated in the second Assembly in 1871, and resigned, being succeeded by Edward Blake, the leader of the Reform Opposition. Blake resigned in 1872, and was succeeded by (Sir) Oliver Mowat of the same political faith. Mowat was successful in the 3rd, 4th, 5th, 6th, 7th and 8th General Elections in 1875, 1879, 1883, 1886, 1890 and 1894 respectively— he resigned in 1896 and was succeeded by Arthur Sturgis Hardy who carried the 9th General Election in 1898, but resigned in 1899 being succeeded by (Sir) George W. Ross. Ross carried the 10th General Election, 1902, but was defeated in the 11th in 1902 and was succeeded by (Sir) James Pliny Whitney, the Leader of Conservative Opposition. Whitney carried the 12th, 13th and 14th General Elections, in 1908, 1911 and 1914 respectively, but died in 1915, and was succeeded by (Sir) William H. Hearst. The term of the 14th Assembly was extended by itself, but Hearst went down to defeat at the 15th General Election. The Farmers' Party being the largest group, their chosen leader, Ernest C. Drury, was sent for: he formed an Administration with the help of the Labour Party which is still (May 1923) in power. [Since this Lecture was delivered, a General Election has been held in Ontario, June, 1923, resulting in a majority for the Conservative Party under G. Howard Ferguson who now, July, 1923, becomes Prime Minister.]

[7]The exercise of this power in the past must not be considered as definitely and finally fixing the practice: Canada is now considerably different from Canada of even a decade ago.

The most striking instance of the exercise of this power was in old Canada. In 1858, the Conservative Government were defeated in the Legislative Assembly (corresponding to the present House of Commons), and Sir Edmund Head, the Governor-General, sent for George Brown, the Leader of the Liberal Opposition, to form a Ministry: the new Ministers were sworn in, and then, not being satisfied with the existing House, asked for a dissolution. Head had given no assurance with reference to dissolving Parliament, and the House had in the absence of the new Ministry given a direct vote of confidence in the old Ministry by a majority of the whole House. The Governor-General said that "the question for His Excellency to decide is not what is advantageous or fair for a particular party, but what upon the whole is the most advantageous and fair for the people of the Province," and he refused to grant a dissolution.

Thereupon Brown and his colleagues resigned—John A. Macdonald's Ministers were recalled and carried on the Government.

A singular expedient, "The Double Shuffle," was adopted to relieve the old Ministry, when taking up the portfolios, from going back to the people for reelection. The Statute, (1857), 20 Vict., C.22, (Can.), authorized Ministers of certain named departments to change their appointments more than once within a month without reelection. Accordingly the nominal Prime Minister was changed and the other Ministers took portfolios different from those which they had held before resignation; and then changed back to their original portfolios.

This "Double Shuffle" was held legal by the Court of Queen's Bench of Upper Canada in McDonell v. Smith, (1859), 17 U. C. Q. B., 310, "although such a proceeding was probably not contemplated by the Act, it was allowed by it," and by the Court of Common Pleas of Upper Canada, Macdonell v. Macdonald, (1859), 8 U. C. C. P., 479, "not even if we thought it would have been wiser policy to make vacating the seat the effect of every acceptance of . . . office . . . can we . . . narrow the interpretation of the words used."

"The Double Shuffle" would not now be imitated, and it is practically certain that no Governor-General would act toward a new Ministry as Sir Edmund Head did toward Brown.

When a new Ministry or an old Ministry in a crisis obtains a dissolution, the practice is to vote just enough supplies to carry on the business of the country till the new Parliament meets.

[8]There are no instances in the Dominion field of dismissal of a Ministry for this reason—there have been two instances in the Provinces. See note 11, p. 44, *post.*

[9]No doubt the power exists in the King, i.e., the Imperial Administration,

to recall a Governor-General—and no doubt in case of improper or unconstitutional conduct on his part or even serious friction with the Canadian statesmen, he would be recalled: but this course has never been followed. The recall of Lord Dufferin was loudly called for in 1873 by some members of one political party because, as was alleged, he was too favorable to the other—but his conduct was unexceptionable, and he won the respect, confidence and even affection of all parties before his term came to an end.

[10] The three instances in England usually adduced are the dismissals in 1784 and 1807 by George III of the Coalition Ministry (which were approved by the electorate) and that in 1834 by William IV of the Melbourne Ministry (which was not)—he "had neither Parliament nor the people with him" as was shown by the ensuing election, for it is only through a Parliament that the people can speak.

[11] The best known instance of disagreement of Lieutenant-Governor and his Ministry is the Letellier case. In 1878, Luc Letellier, the Lieutenant-Governor of the Province of Quebec, dismissed his Ministry—he alleged that they paid no proper attention to his suggestions, that they had, as he believed, corruptly and for political purposes promoted certain lavish expenditures of public money and had caused to be passed a Railway Act giving to themselves instead of to the Courts the power to determine the rights of claimants—he repeatedly warned them but in vain, and he consequently dismissed them. He then called upon Joly the leader of the Opposition to form a Ministry, which he did: the new Ministry was granted a dissolution and at the ensuing election the parties were almost evenly balanced. But Joly was able to carry on and even to obtain a vote of confidence though this was by a majority of only one. Some members of the dismissed Ministry sent in a Petition to the Governor-General for the dismissal of Letellier and there were statements and counterstatements. The Dominion Ministry took no action and a motion in the House of Commons (to whom as well as to the Senate the papers had been sent without comment) that Letellier's dismissal of the Ministry was unwise and subversive of the principles of responsible government was defeated by a large majority—the Senate, however, carried a similar motion. The votes in each House were on strictly party lines.

The Dominion Parliament being about to the end of its statutory life—five years—was dissolved, and at the ensuing General Election a majority of the Opposition Party was returned: a new Ministry came in, 1879, and the motion which had been defeated in the House of Commons in 1878 was now carried by a large majority—thereupon the new Ministry informed the Governor-General, the Marquis of Lorne, that "the usefulness of M. Letellier as Lieutenant-Governor was gone," and advised his removal. The Governor-General did not approve, thinking such a proceeding would set a dangerous precedent, and it was arranged to refer the matter to the Imperial Administration. That Government said that the Lieutenant-Governor had the constitutional right to dismiss his Ministers but that in deciding whether such a course warranted his removal from office the Governor-General must act "by and with the advice of his Ministers." The Ottawa Administration adhered to their previous advice and Letellier was removed, July, 1874, the cause assigned being that after the vote of the two Houses of Parliament his usefulness as Lieutenant-Governor was gone.

These proceedings were all at a time of great political excitement and animosity. Letellier was of the same political party as the Ottawa Ministry in 1878: he dismissed a Ministry of the opposite party which then in Opposition at Ottawa achieved power in 1879. It is probable that no future dismissal will ever take place on such grounds.

Another case occurred in Quebec in 1891—Lieutenant-Governor Angers on the Interim Report of two out of three Judges appointed as a Royal Commission to examine into alleged improprieties of the Quebec Ministry in connection with a certain Railway (the third Commissioner was ill) dismissed the Ministry headed by M. Mercier: the facts found in the Report were different in some respects from the statements of Mercier to the Lieutenant-Governor and he without waiting for a full Report from the Commission said "that the Ministry is not in a position to advise the representative of the Crown wisely, disinterestedly and faithfully." M. de Boucherville was sent for to form and did form a new Ministry—they advised a dissolution and, although the existing Assembly had just come from the people and had never met, a General Election was ordered. This resulted in a complete victory for the new Government, and Lieutenant-Governor Angers was thus justified by the people.

Had he failed of justification, his conduct would still have been perfectly constitutional: probably at the present time, a Lieutenant-Governor would not act so peremptorily but would await the full Report of the three judges.

No other Provincial Governments have actually been dismissed; but in 1915, in Manitoba, the Lieutenant-Governor, Sir Douglas Cameron, insisting upon a Royal Commission to examine into certain charges of fraud in connection with public buildings, and the Commission reporting overpayments to the knowledge of a Government architect, the Ministry resigned, a new Ministry was formed which went to the country and was returned with a very large majority.

[12] In the Letellier case (see preceding note) the Lieutenant-Governor claimed that as the direct and personal representative of the Sovereign he was "irresponsible for acts performed within the legitimate sphere of duties prescribed to him by the B. N. A. Act": but this claim was denied by the Dominion Government and the Imperial authorities.

[13] B. N. A. sec. 58 provides that he is to be appointed by the Governor-General-in-Council: sec. 59 that he "shall hold office during the pleasure of the Governor-General." By reason of the difference in the terminology, Prime Minister Joly in the Letellier case (see note 11 *supra*) contended that the dismissal must be the act of the Governor-General personally. This contention was not allowed to prevail—the Imperial authorities declaring specifically that in deciding whether the conduct of a Lieutenant-Governor was such as to merit dismissal the Governor-General must act by and with the advice of his Ministers.

[14] In fact, of course, the House of Commons and in the ultimate result the electorate are the final judges—the Ministry being responsible to the House

in this as in all other matters. Whether the Lieutenant-Governor has acted so arbitrarily, partially or wrongfully in any other respect as to deserve dismissal is to be determined in the first place by the Dominion Ministry, the propriety of their action is determined by the House of Commons (if necessary by a formal vote) and the action of the House of Commons may be made an issue in the General Election.

[15] See note 11 *suprâ*.

[16] The Senate cannot constitutionally amend a money Bill though it can reject it *in toto*. If a money Bill from the Commons is sent back from the Senate with amendments it is usual at the present time, to send it back to the Senate with reasons for disagreeing with the amendments so that the Senate may withdraw them—the strict course followed until recently was to lay the Bill aside. If a Bill be sent down by the Senate containing a clause or clauses involving the expenditure of public money, etc. the strict course is to lay it aside; at the present time, if it is necessary or convenient to introduce in the Senate a Bill containing clauses involving public expenditure, it is usual to print the clauses in the Bill, strike them out in Committee and send the Bill to the Commons with the clauses in red ink or italics.

[17] On one occasion in England the consent of the Crown was given to a private member of the House of Commons to introduce certain Resolutions in respect of public expenditure: 187 English Hansard (3) p. 1667: but no case of the kind has ever occurred in Canada nor is it at all probable that such will ever occur. All that can be said is that it is not impossible.

[18] There are certain Rules as to Bills, procedure etc., of each House which I do not detail here—they form no part of the Constitution.

[19] When Britain actually ruled Canada it was the custom to direct the Governor-General (in the Royal Instructions) to reserve for the Sovereign's pleasure certain classes of Bills—this was put an end to in 1878, and since that time there has not even been any semblance of authority for such a course. Before Confederation, the practice was very common: but since that event there has been no instance of the kind except in such special classes of cases.

The Royal Assent is in practice given in the Senate Chamber in presence of both Houses specially called together for the purpose—sometimes the Deputy Governor gives the formal assent.

In 1868, a Bill reducing to £6500 the Governor-General's salary of £10,000 as fixed by the B. N. A. Act, sec. 105, "unless altered by the Parliament of Canada" was reserved by Viscount Monck—the Colonial Secretary notified Lord Monck that Her Majesty would be advised not to give Her assent: in the next year the Canadian Parliament passed an Act, (1869), 32, 33, Vict., C. CLXXIV (Dom.) (see Dominion Statutes for 1870, p. iii) fixing the salary at £10,000 or $48,666.63: the Bill was reserved under the existing Instructions (now altered) and received the Royal Assent. A Bill in 1874 respecting Copyright reserved as repugnant to an Imperial Act was refused the Royal Assent: as was a Bill in 1874 respecting Marine Telegraphs. All other Bills reserved including certain Divorce Bills have received the Royal Assent, B. N. A. Act, sect. 56.

[21] In 1873, a charge had been made against the Ministry of Canada of receiving large subscriptions for election funds from a Company formed to build a Canadian Pacific Railway. A Bill was passed by both Houses providing for the examination under oath of witnesses before Committees of either House: the Governor-General gave the Royal Assent but in his despatch he enclosed a memorandum from the Minister of Justice (who was also Prime Minister) expressing doubt of the power of the Canadian Parliament to pass it and desiring that the Home Administration should consider the question. The matter was laid before the Law Officers of the Crown in England who advised that the legislation was *ultra vires* the Dominion Parliament and it was disallowed.

This is the only instance since Confederation of the exercise by the Crown of the statutory right of disallowance.

[22] B. N. A. Act, secs. 53, 90: Rev. St. Que. (1888), Sec. 111.

[23] For some time there was a theoretical but hardly practical question as to whether the Governor-General in this regard must be guided solely by the advice of the Dominion Ministry or might and, indeed, should act on his individual discretion; but it may be considered settled that he has no discretion in the matter. In fact no Governor-General in Canada has since Confederation decided upon the allowance or disallowance of Provincial laws except on the advice of his Ministers—and no Governor-General has ever asserted or even suggested a claim to do so.

[24] See Chapter II, note 26, p. 29, *supra*.

[25] Every Province has Home Rule; and the Legislature should answer to the people of its own Province for the exercise of its powers; where it has clearly exceeded its powers it would be oppressive to compel those aggrieved to have it declared *ultra vires* at their own expense; and moreover the Dominion cannot justify permitting anybody to trench on its domain.

Perhaps the practice may be considered to have been stated rather too widely in the text; a short history may be of interest. June 8, 1868, less than a year after Confederation, the first Prime Minister of Canada, Sir John A. Macdonald laid down four grounds on which disallowance of Provincial Acts was properly effected.

(1) As being altogether illegal or unconstitutional.

(2) As illegal or unconstitutional in part.

(3) In cases of concurrent jurisdiction as clashing with the legislation of the General Parliament.

(4) As affecting the interests of the Dominion generally.

In his report on the British Columbia Statute, "The Vancouver Island Settlers' Rights Act, 1904," Mr. Doherty, Minister of Justice in Sir Robert Borden's Cabinet, appears to believe that there are other grounds for disallowance; he speaks as follows:

"It will be perceived by review of the reports of the Minister of Justice from the Union to the present time, that there has been great reluctance to interfere with provincial legislation, and that notwithstanding a considerable number of cases in which disallowance was sought upon established grounds. Provincial legislation has not been generally disallowed by reason merely of the injustice of its provisions. Cases are not lacking, however, in which disallowance has been avoided by reason of amendments undertaken by the local authorities, upon the suggestion of the Ministers of Justice, to remedy the complaints against the original Acts; and certainly the constitutional propriety and duty of reviewing provincial legislation upon its merits when it is the subject of serious complaint has been maintained by every succeeding Minister of Justice from the time of the Union, save only the immediate predecessor of the undersigned who suggested in effect that the power had become obsolete. In the opinion of the undersigned the power is unquestionable and remains in full vigour. Indeed the very careful consideration which the Ministers have been accustomed to give to applications presented from time to time for disallowance depending upon reasons of inequality or hardship is inconsistent with any other view."

The immediate predecessor of Mr. Doherty referred to is the Sir Allen B. Aylesworth; Sir Allen reporting on "An Act respecting Cobalt Lake and Kerr Lake," Statutes of Ontario, 1907, held that as the Act did not fall within any of the four grounds laid down by Sir John A. Macdonald, disallowance was not in order.

A rather interesting case of disallowance occurred in connection with the Statutes of Nova Scotia, Chapters 14 and 40, 1922, respecting the Rule of the Road. These Statutes were not disallowed on grounds of *ultra vires*, conflict or injustice but because they conflicted with each other. The Minister of Justice in his report on these Statutes found the case to be without precedent. The action of the Dominion Administration in advising disallowance was really taken at the instance of the Nova Scotia Administration.

[26] Anyone affected by a Provincial measure may petition for its disallowance at Ottawa: in some cases parties interested are heard by Counsel before the Minister of Justice. The most recent case of such petition was in the case of Roberts mentioned in Chapter I, note 16, p. 16, *ante*.

[27] The King is considered a part of the Parliament of Canada and all Statutes are in the following form:

"His Majesty by and with the advice and consent of the Senate and House of Commons of Canada, enacts as follows"—

The form in the Imperial Parliament at Westminster reads:

"Be it enacted by the King's Most Excellent Majesty by and with the advice and consent of the Lords Spiritual and Temporal and Commons in this present Parliament assembled and by the authority of the same, as follows"—

In the Provinces of Ontario, Manitoba, Alberta, British Columbia:

"His Majesty by and with the advice and consent of the Legislative Assembly of the Province of   enacts as follows"—

In the Province of Saskatchewan:

"His Majesty by and with the advice and consent of the Legislative Assembly of Saskatchewan enacts as follows"—

In the Province of New Brunswick:
"Be it enacted by the Lieutenant-Governor and Legislative Assembly as follows"—
In the Province of Prince Edward Island:
"Be it enacted by the Lieutenant-Governor and Legislative Assembly of the Province of Prince Edward Island as follows"—
Of the bicameral Provinces in Quebec:
"His Majesty by and with the advice and Consent of the Legislative Council and Legislative Assembly of Quebec, enacts as follows"—
and in New Brunswick:
"Be it enacted by the Governor, Council and Assembly as follows"—
Notwithstanding the difference in terminology, the King is a part of every Provincial Legislature: and it is the Royal assent that is given.
In the Yukon Territory:
"The Commissioner of the Yukon Territory by and with the consent of the Council of the said Territory enacts as follows".

NOTE ON THE TERRITORIES

Before leaving the subject of legislation it will be well to show how the Territories are legislated for, as their legislative bodies are not the same as those of the nine Provinces.

THE YUKON TERRITORY

The Yukon Territory in the northwestern corner of Canada is not a Province and has not Provincial status or powers.

Organized in 1898 as a Territory, it has seen several changes made in its Constitution; it is proposed, here, to state its present position with the caution that this may be modified at any time by the Parliament of Canada.

The Governor-in-Council at Ottawa appoints by an instrument under the Great Seal, a chief executive officer styled and known as the Commissioner of the Yukon Territory, R. S. C. (1906) C. 63, s. 4; and the Governor-in-Council may appoint an Administrator to act in the absence, illness or other inability of the Commissioner, (1907), 6. 7 Edward VII, C. 53 (Dom.); (1908) 7, 8 Edward VII, C. 76 (Dom.).

There is a Council composed of three persons elected on a franchise prescribed by the Commissioner, (1909) 9, 10 Geo. V., C. 9, (Can.); R. S. C., (1906), C. 63, s. 9.

The Council continues for three years subject to the right of the Commissioner to dissolve it at any time and cause a new Council to be elected.

The Council meets at least once a year and, sitting separately from the Commissioner, passes Bills and presents them to the Commissioner for his assent—he may approve or disapprove of any of such Bills or reserve them for the assent of the Governor-General-in-Council. No money Bill, Vote, Resolution or Address can be considered without having been first recommended by the Commissioner—the members of the Council are paid $400 per annum and traveling expenses.

Power was given the Governor-in-Council by the Act, (1918) 8, 9 Geo. V., C. 50, to abolish the elective Council and substitute one composed of two or more members appointed by the Governor-in-Council—but this power has not been exercised.

LEGISLATIVE POWERS

The legislative powers of the Council, who (as has been said) sit apart from the Commissioner, are not quite so broad as those of the Provincial Legislatures—the subjects of legislation are enumerated in the R. S. C., (1906), C. 63, 2. 12:

(a) The establishment and tenure of territorial offices and the appointment and payment of territorial officers out of territorial revenues;

(b) The establishment, maintenance and management of prisons in and for the Territory, the expense thereof being payable out of territorial revenues;

(c) Municipal institutions in the Territory;

(d) Shop, saloon, tavern, auctioneer and other licenses in order to raise a revenue for territorial or municipal purposes;

(e) The incorporation of companies with territorial objects, excepting railway companies (not including tramway and street railway companies) and steamboat, canal, telegraph and irrigation companies;

(f) The solemnization of marriage in the Territory;

(g) Property and civil rights in the Territory;

(h) The administration of justice in the Territory, including the constitution, organization and maintenance of territorial courts of civil jurisdiction, including procedure therein, but not including the appointment of judicial officers, or the constitution, organization and maintenance of courts of criminal jurisdiction, or procedure in criminal matters;

(i) The defining of the powers, duties and obligations of sheriffs and clerks of the courts and their respective deputies;

(j) The conferring on territorial courts of jurisdiction in matters of alimony;

(k) The imposition of punishment by fine, penalty or imprisonment, for enforcing any territorial ordinances;

(l) The expenditure of territorial funds and such portion of any moneys appropriated by Parliament for the Territory as the Commissioner is authorized to expend by and with the advice of the Council or of any committee thereof;

(m) Generally, all matters of a merely local or private nature in the Territory.

Also for

(a) imposing taxes for any purpose within his jurisdiction;

(b) respecting the summoning of juries and the enforcement of the attendance or jurors for the trial of civil and criminal cases and respecting the payment of the costs and expenses in connection therewith;

(c) for the control and regulation of the sale of and traffic in intoxicating liquor in the Territory, subject to the provisions of any ordinance of the

Governor-in-Council and notwithstanding anything to the contrary in any Act of Parliament;

(d) for the preservation of game in the Territory.

Responsible Government has not yet been granted to the people of the Yukon.

COURTS

The Yukon has its own Territorial Court at present with one Judge (formerly with three), a Barrister of at least ten years standing, removable on Address by the two Houses of Parliament. This Court has full civil and criminal jurisdiction; the Court of Appeal of British Columbia is the Court of Appeal for the Territory.

Police Magistrates are also appointed by the Governor-in-Council with somewhat large jurisdiction.

THE NORTH WEST TERRITORIES

The Governor-General-in-Council appoints for the "North West Territories" a chief executive officer styled and known as the Commissioner of the North West Territory, R. S. C., (1906), C., C. 62, s. 3: he is to administer the government under instructions from time to time given him from the Minister of the Interior, (1907), 6, 7 Edw. VII, C. 32, s. 4 (2) (Dom.).

COUNCIL

There is a Council to aid the Commissioner in the administration of the Territories, R. S. C., (1906), C. 62, s. 6, consisting of six persons appointed by the Governor-General-in-Council; one of these may be and in fact is appointed Deputy Commissioner with the powers of the Commissioner in his absence, (1921), 11, 12 Geo. V., C. 40, (Dom.).

LEGISLATIVE POWERS OF COMMISSIONER IN COUNCIL

The Commissioner sits with the Council in Ottawa and they make ordinances—the legislative power is somewhat large and is thus laid down in the R. S. C. (1906) C. 62, s. 8:

(a) Direct taxation within the Territories in order to raise a revenue for territorial or municipal or local purposes;

(b) The establishment and tenure of territorial offices and the appointment and payment of territorial officers out of territorial revenues;

(c) The establishment, maintenance and management of prisons in and for the Territories, the expense thereof being payable out of territorial revenues;

(d) Municipal institutions in the Territories, including the incorporation and powers, not inconsistent with any Act of Parliament, or irrigation districts, that is to say, associations of the land owners, and persons interested in the lands, in any district or tract of land for the purpose of constructing and operating irrigation works for the benefit of such lands;

(e) The closing up or varying the direction of any road allowance, or of any trail which has been transferred to the Territories, and the opening and establishing of any new highway instead of any road or trail so closed, and the disposition of the land in any such road or trail;

(f) Shop, saloon, tavern, auctioneer and other licenses, in order to raise a revenue for territorial or municipal purposes;

(g) The incorporation of companies with territorial objects, excepting railway companies (not including tramway and street railway companies) and steamboat, canal, telegraph and irrigation companies;

(h) The solemnization of marriage in the Territories;

(i) Property and civil rights in the Territories;

(j) The administration of justice in the Territories, including the constitution, organization and maintenance of territorial courts of civil jurisdiction, and procedure in such courts, but not including the appointment of any judicial officers or the constitution, organization and maintenance of courts of criminal jurisdiction, or procedure in criminal matters;

(k) The mode of calling juries, other than grand juries, in criminal as well as civil cases, and when and by whom and the manner in which they may be summoned or taken, and all matters relating to the same;

(l) The defining of the powers, duties and obligations of sheriffs and clerks of the courts and their respective deputies;

(m) The conferring on territorial courts of jurisdiction in matters of alimony;

(n) The imposition of punishment by fine, penalty or imprisonment, for enforcing any territorial ordinances;

(o) The expenditure of territorial funds and such portion of any moneys appropriated by Parliament for the Territories as the Commissioner in Council is authorized to expend;

(p) Generally, all matters of a merely local or private nature in the Territories.

Nothing like Responsible Government is given to the Territories; the Legislative body, the Council, does not even sit apart from the Executive or within the Territories.

COURTS

The Northwest Territories have no Courts presided over by Judges. The Governor-in-Council appoints stipendiary Magistrates who have substantially the same powers as a Superior Court Judge, civil and criminal. The Superior Courts of the adjoining Provinces, Ontario, Manitoba, Saskatchewan, Alberta and British Columbia are given civil jurisdiction in certain parts of the Territories, (1908), 7, 8 Edw. VII, C. 49 (Dom.).

CHAPTER IV

JUDICATURE

The B. N. A. Act allots to the Provinces "The Administration of Justice in the Province including the Constitution, Maintenance and Organization of Provincial Courts, both of Civil and Criminal Jurisdiction, and including Procedure in Civil matters in those Courts."

To the Dominion, the Act allots "The Criminal Law except the Constitution of Courts of Criminal Jurisdiction but including the Procedure in Criminal matters."

Further, "the Governor-General shall appoint the Judges of the Superior District and County Courts in each Province, except those of the Courts of Probate in Nova Scotia and New Brunswick." [1] Consequently each Province erects such and so many Courts as it sees fit, Superior or Inferior, Trial or Appellate, but the Dominion appoints the Judges if the Courts are Superior, District or County Courts.

Moreover, the Dominion was authorized by the B. N. A. Act to "provide for the constitution, maintenance and organization of a Court of Appeal for Canada, and for the establishment of any additional Courts for the better administration of the laws of Canada"; and has done so in the Supreme Court of Canada and the Exchequer Court of Canada. [2]

Inferior judicial officers, Police Magistrates and Justices of the Peace, are appointed by the Province, as are Surrogate and Probate Judges. [3]

All Judges appointed by the Dominion are selected from the Bar of the Province for which they are appointed. [4]

The Salaries, Allowances and Pensions of all Judges appointed by the Dominion are paid by the Dominion—of all judicial officers appointed by the Province, by the Province.[5]

The appointment of all judicial officers is during good behavior—Judges of the Superior Courts can be removed by the Governor-General only on an Address of both Houses of Parliament; District and County Court Judges may be removed without such Address, and provincially-appointed officers may be removed by the Lieutenant-Governor.[6]

The ultimate appellate tribunal for Canada is the Judicial Committee of the (Imperial) Privy Council—the ultimate Court of Appeal for the whole British Commonwealth, except England, Scotland and Ireland.[7]

MUNICIPAL SYSTEMS

The B. N. A. Act allots to the Provinces legislation in relation to Municipal Institutions within the Province;[8] and no small part of the prosperity and happiness of the people depends on municipal institutions.

As the various Provinces have full power in the premises, the Municipal Institutions are not the same throughout the Dominion.

Those of Quebec are *sui generis*; those of the Maritime Provinces, Nova Scotia and New Brunswick resemble each other more closely than either resembles those of Ontario. The Ontario System has been to a great extent the model for those of the new Provinces, Manitoba, Saskatchewan and Alberta and, to a somewhat less degree, for British Columbia.

MUNICIPAL INSTITUTIONS IN ONTARIO

All the organized parts of Ontario are divided into Counties, the Counties into Cities, Towns and Villages in thickly inhabited districts and into Townships in rural districts. For municipal purposes, the Cities and many of the Towns are separate from the Counties—Towns and Villages not separate from the Counties have much the same government as the Townships. The inhabitants of all Counties,

Cities, Towns, Villages and Townships are made Bodies
Corporate; and each has its own Municipal Council elected
annually by the people. The powers of these Municipal
Councils are very great in local matters; and they have been
considered admirable schools for public life.[9]

GENERAL HISTORICAL SKETCH

The Constitutional History of Canada readily divides
itself into seven Periods—(I use the word Canada in the
historical not the geographical sense, omitting a great part
of the present Canada for the sake of brevity).

FIRST PERIOD (1534 TO 1759-60), FRENCH PERIOD

During the French period in Canada, Nouvelle France,
the King's Lieutenant had at first very extensive powers to
make laws and to appoint civil and military officers, powers
not different in kind and not very different in extent from
those of the King of France himself. Richelieu, in 1627, gave
the country over to the care of the "Company of One
Hundred Associates", but this Régime lasted only till 1663;
in 1664 the "Company of the West Indies" succeeded and in
1674 the King resumed a considerable part of the deputed
power. It is not of importance here to trace the various
changes—as the French Régime has left no trace in the
present Constitution.[10]

SECOND PERIOD (1759-60 TO 1763-4), RÉGIME MILITAIRE

On the Conquest of Canada by the British, completed in
1760 but begun at Quebec the previous year, the country
passed under military rule, and there ensued what is called
the Régime Militatire or Règne Militaire. This military
régime has been painted in very dark colors by some
writers; but in fact it seems to have been as mild and con-
siderate as any military rule could well be.

Canada was ceded to Britain by the Treaty of Paris,[11]

concluded February 10, 1763, which allowed eighteen months for any French who were so disposed to depart from Canada.

THIRD PERIOD (1763-4 TO 1774), TRANSITION PERIOD

October 7, 1763, a Royal Proclamation was issued stating that the King had erected (*inter alia*) a "Government of Quebec," running from the River St. John, west at Labrador, to a line drawn from the south end of Lake Nipissing to the place at which the Parallel of 45° North Latitude crosses the St. Lawrence. A Governor-in-Chief was appointed (General James Murray) and given Instructions as well as a Commission. There was also provision made for a Council composed at first of four officials selected by the Home Administration and eight to be chosen by the Governor "from amongst the most considerable of the Inhabitants of or Persons of Property" in the Province. As these Councillors were required to take the Declaration against Popery prescribed by the Statute passed in the reign of Charles II, no Roman Catholic could be a Councillor.

While the Proclamation contemplated that a General Assembly should be summoned as soon as the situation and circumstances of the Province would admit, in the meantime the Governor with the advice and consent of the Council could establish Courts of Justice and he could without such advice and consent, appoint Judges, Justices of the Peace, Sheriffs, etc.

No Civil Courts were in fact established until after the lapse of the eighteen months allowed for anyone so desiring to leave Canada; but Courts, civil and criminal, were established by an Ordinance, made by the Governor "by and with the Advice, Consent and Assistance of His Majesty's Council," September 17, 1764.[12]

No Assembly was summoned during this period; and the country was governed by the Governor assisted in certain matters by the appointed Council. The Council sat with and under the presidency of the Governor, and he was the ultimate authority upon whom the responsibility for the government of the Province was cast.

This state of affairs finds a not very imperfect parallel in the North West Territories at the present time—this being an atavistic reversion for a particular part of Canada to the first form of civil government in Canada under Britain.[13]

FOURTH PERIOD (1774 TO 1791), THE QUEBEC ACT

The project of summoning an Assembly proved abortive—the Protestant English-speaking inhabitants were a very small part of the whole population and no Roman Catholic could take the oaths at that time required of all legislators. At length, the Imperial Parliament passed the celebrated Quebec Act in 1774, which reintroduced the former French Civil law; this Act increased the extent of Quebec to the West and South West, and made no provision for an Assembly, declaring that "it is at present inexpedient to call an Assembly."

The King was to appoint a Council of persons resident in the Province not exceeding twenty-three or less than seventeen in number "which Council . . . or the major part thereof shall have power and authority to make Ordinances for the peace, welfare and good government of the Province, with the consent of His Majesty's Governor"—the King to have the right to disallow any Ordinance.

This contemplated the Council sitting as a body apart from the Governor, and passing Ordinances to be then submitted to the Governor for his consent; consequently in all Ordinances before the Quebec Act the terminology employed is "Given by His Excellency . . . Governor-in-Chief . . . In Council . . ."; thereafter "Ordained and enacted . . . and passed in Council under the Great Seal of the Province. . . ."

The responsibility for legislation was laid upon the Council, but the Governor was not relieved from responsibility in giving his consent to legislation—in fact, all the Governors took an active part in respect to Ordinances.

It will be observed that this system bears a very close resemblance to the original system of the Yukon, a nominated Council charged with legislation and a Governor to give or refuse consent.

The Quebec Act established full religious tolerance and abolished the necessity to take the oaths offensive to Roman Catholics; a new form of oath was given which could be taken by those of that religion.[14]

The close of the Revolutionary War and the recognition of the Independence of the United States brought into the country many English-speaking and (in general) Protestant immigrants from the Thirteen Colonies; they did not like French laws and customs and detested government by non-elective bodies. There was little or no hope of the English and French working together harmoniously and it was decided to divide the Province of Quebec into two Provinces with separate Legislatures.[15]

FIFTH PERIOD (1791 TO 1841), THE CANADA ACT

The formal division of the Province of Quebec into Upper Canada and Lower Canada was by Order-in-Council; but provision for the government of the two new Provinces was made by the Canada or Constitutional Act of 1791.[16]

This Act provided for a Legislative Council and a Legislative Assembly in each Province, the former appointed for life by the Governor,[17] the latter elected by the people—the persons appointed by the Governor to be stated by the Sovereign.[18]

For Upper Canada there were to be not less than seven members in the Legislative Council; for Lower Canada not less than fifteen; with these and their selection the people of the Provinces had nothing to do; and the Governor appointed the Speaker of the Legislative Council.

The Legislative Assembly in Upper Canada was to consist of at least sixteen members, in Lower Canada of at least fifty.

The Houses sat separately and passed Bills; when a Bill was presented for His Majesty's assent to the Governor, etc., he might (1) assent to the Bill (2) withold the King's assent or (3) reserve it for the signification of His Majesty's pleasure.[19]

In the Instructions to the Governor, he was directed as to his duties in this respect—certain forms were to be observed in the Bills, each different matter was to be dealt with in a different Bill, no clause inserted foreign to the title, no general repeal, etc.; and if any Bill should be passed respecting private property without reserving the rights of the Crown it was to be reserved for the King's pleasure. Certain other Bills were to be reserved and assent refused to Bills for naturalization of Aliens, Divorce[20], and establishing title to land bought from Aliens.

In this period the Governor not only took an active personal part in the administration of the Province but also exercised his personal and individual judgment in respect of legislation as the Governor of an American State does to this day; scores of Bills were reserved during this period. He had an Executive Council selected as a rule by himself, and receiving appointment from the Home Administration, but he was at liberty to disregard their advice and frequently did so. This Council was in no way responsible to the people or their representatives in the Assembly, but only to the Governor and in the last result to the King as the American Cabinet at Washington is to the President.

An agitation sprang up in both Provinces for Responsible Government, and after a short and abortive Rebellion[21] in 1837-8, Lord Durham was appointed Governor-General and made a personal investigation and Report.

The result was a Union of the two Canadas.

SIXTH PERIOD (1841 TO 1867), UNION ACT

By the Union Act of 1840,[22] the two Canadas were united into the Province of Canada with a Governor, a Legislative Council and a Legislative Assembly—not less than twenty Councillors were appointed by the Crown and the Assemblymen elected by the people.

An Executive Council was also provided for to be appointed by Her Majesty.

When a Bill was presented to the Governor, he had the same rights as before and the same as are now contained in the B. N. A. Act; the Home Administration could then as now disallow any Act within two years.

There was no outward change in the frame of the Constitution; but the intention was to give Canada Responsible Government; and in a few years Responsible Government was firmly established and Canada ruled herself.

In the matter of Tariff legislation the interference of the Home Government did not disappear till 1859.

SEVENTH PERIOD (1867—   ), THE DOMINION

We have already described the Constitution in this period.

A few salient facts may be adduced as evidencing the evolution of Canada during this period.

Canada, being mistress in her own house, having full control over her own country both internally and in tariff relations with the world at large, was still without influence in respect of the remainder of the British Empire.

1887.

In 1887 a great step forward was made. Then was held the first Colonial Conference of the Prime Minister of Britain and the Prime Ministers of the self-governing Dominions to confer on matters of common interest to the British world.[23]

Accordingly, from and after 1887, Canada not only was

in full control of her own affairs, but she advised on matters affecting the whole Empire.

1897.

In 1897, another step forward was made. Canada proposed to give British goods a preference by reducing the customs dues below those of goods of other origin. Germany and Belgium protested; they had treaties with Britain entitling them to as favorable a tariff as any other country in Britain and her dependencies. Canada was—and, for that matter, is,—in the theory of international law, a Dependency of Britain; Germany and Belgium were technically right, and their right was acknowledged by Canada. But at the meeting of the Colonial Conference in 1897, Sir Wilfrid Laurier, our Prime Minister, insisted that the obnoxious treaties should be denounced, and denounced they were; whereupon the "British Preference" became a fact.[24]

Canada thus passed beyond her former limits; not only did she frame her own tariff, she caused the Mother Country to change her tariff treaty arrangements.

1907.

In 1907, the Colonial Conference came to an end. It was seen and felt that the word "Colonial" was a misnomer; the status of Colony was outgrown, the Dominions were self-governing in fact whatever the form. Consequently there was formed a new body under the name of the Imperial Conference.[25]

Then came the war.

Canada did not delay a minute—the Atlantic cable carried the message, "The last man and the last dollar."

Canada raised her own forces, equipped them with Canadian guns, Canadian munitions, cared for them, and pays the pensions of wounded survivor and widow and child of the honored dead. Sixty thousand Canadian dead and three times as many wounded prove how Canada acquitted herself. England could not call upon her for a soldier, a ship, an ounce of supplies, a cent of money; nor did she fight for England. She poured out her money like water, her men died in tens of thousands for a struggle she called and calls her own, because she believed and believes it to be for humanity at large and for her own chosen form of civilization. And Britain knows. Since the War began, no responsible British statesman has ever spoken of Canada as a Colony.[26]

1917.

Canadians were dying by thousands, and it was felt that Canada should have some say in the conduct of the War. And this is what was done:

"In 1917 the Prime Minister of Great Britain called together the ministers of the self-governing Dominions for consultation on vital matters of policy relating to the prosecution of the war. They met as equals as Prime Ministers of the nations of the Empire, to discuss matters of common concern to the whole Empire. Great Britain recognized that, with the growth of power and influence of the Dominions, the time had come when the Government of Great Britain should frankly recognize that the Dominions had ceased to be in any sense states dependent upon the Mother Country, and had become sister Nations, standing on an equality with the Mother Country."[27]

The War ended, Canada demanded as a right to be a party to the Treaty of Peace—her representatives are taking an honorable part in the League of Nations.[28]

The expression "British Dominions" has taken on a new and permanent connotation. It no longer means territory under the dominion of the British Isles; it means Dominions possessed by the British people within the borders of the Dominions themselves; no adjunct to any other people, British or foreign.[29]

So stands Canada today, able and willing to stand alone if she must, but ardently desiring the respect and esteem of the world at large and especially of the rest of the English-speaking world—not least her near neighbor and kin, the

United States of America, with whom she has lived in peace for more than a century—*sit aeterna*.

Old names persist, old ceremonies survive—but it is the glory of our unwritten constitution that we build more stately mansions on the old foundations, we graft new and fruitful shoots on the old stock, we fill with a new and beautiful life the old ceremonies and forms.

The "New British Empire", the "British Commonwealth", is the triumph of the unwritten constitution, which none who know not the virtues of an unwritten constitution can understand. No people but the English-speaking Anglo-Saxon-Celt could elaborate or even conceive of such a scheme.

Legislation there must be to make the form in some degree accord with the fact. In a few months or years there may be a Convention or Conference of statesmen from all parts of the far-flung British world, whose task it will be to frame a Constitution that all may read, with word married to fact. We are, and we intend to continue members of a British League of Nations inside the Empire in a separate, distinct and intimate relationship of our own with the United Kingdom and the other Dominions.

That will not be permitted to interfere with our absolute right to sit as a separate member in international conferences by the side of the United Kingdom, backing her when we so decide and opposing her (as we have done already more than once) when we judge it proper so to do.

NOTES TO CHAPTER IV

[1] B. N. A. Act, secs. 92 (14); 91 (27); 96.

In Ontario, the Surrogate Courts which are charged with wills, probate, administration, etc., are not within the category of Courts whose Judges are to be appointed by the Dominion.

[2] B. N. A. Act, sec. 101.

The Supreme Court of Canada and the Exchequer Court of Canada constituted by the Act, (1875), 38 Vict., C. 11, (Dom.)—the Judges (a Chief Justice and five Puisné Justices) of the Supreme Court to be Judges of the

Exchequer Court. The Supreme Court is an Appellate Court, while the Exchequer Court is a Court of original jurisdiction.

The work of the Supreme Court becoming great, the Exchequer Court was given a separate Judge by the Act, (1887), 50, 51 Vict., C. 16, (Dom.); an Assistant Judge was provided for by the Act, (1912), 2 Geo. V., C. 21, (Dom.) and the Act, (1920), 10, 11 Geo. V., C. 26, makes the Judge and Assistant Judge, President and Puisné Judge respectively.

³The Province of Quebec in 1888 purported to erect a "District Magistrates' Court" in Montreal, presided over by Justices appointed by the Lieutenant-Governor; the Act purported to abolish the Circuit Court at Montreal presided over by Supreme Court Judges appointed by the Governor-General. This Act was disallowed—whereupon in 1889, the Province created a Magistrates' Court for the District of Montreal—this was *intra vires* and was not disallowed.

⁴B. N. A. Act, secs. 97, 98—if the laws relating to Property and Civil Rights in Ontario, Nova Scotia and New Brunswick and the Procedure in the Courts are made uniform, the Judges for the Courts of any of these Provinces may be selected from the Bar of any of them—that will not be till the Greek Kalends.

In Ontario, a Barrister-at-law to be appointed Judge of the Supreme Court (our only Superior Court) must have been a member of the Bar of Ontario for ten years; to be appointed Judge of a County or District Court he must have been for seven years such member.

⁵Objection has been taken by the Dominion to any increase in the salary or emolument of Judges by a Province—and such increase has been declared *ultra vires* a Province by the Imperial Law officers of the Crown; but in Ontario by the Act, R. S. O., (1914), C. 57, every Judge of the Supreme Court receives $1,000 per annum as compensation for any services which he is called upon to render by any Act of the Legislature in addition to his ordinary duties—these services are at the present time confined to the examination of and report upon legislation, actual or proposed.

⁶In the case of District and County Court Judges, the practice in case of complaint is to appoint a Commission of two Superior Court Judges to enquire and report—in the two cases with which I am familiar the Judges (both charged with inebriety) resigned before the Commission actually reported. There have been no charges against a Judge in Canada of corruption or the like, since long before Confederation.

Before 1857, there was no statutory provision in Upper Canada for the investigation of charges against County Court Judges; but in that year by the Statute, (1857), 20 Vict., C. 58, (Can.) a Court of Impeachment was erected composed of the Heads of the Superior Courts of Law and Equity (two Chief Justices and the Chancellor) for such purpose, C. S., U. C., (1859), C. 14—this has long been obsolete.

Before 1849 there was nothing to prevent the removal of Superior Court Judges in Upper or Lower Canada by the Governor: in that year, the Act, (1849), 12 Vict., C. 63, (Can.) required an Address from both Houses of the Legislature—that has been the law ever since.

Before 1849, two Judges were "amoved" in Upper Canada—Mr. Justice Robert Thorpe, an Irishman, in 1807, and Mr. Justice John Walpole Willis, an Englishman, in 1828; their conduct was wholly inexcusable; there has been none since 1828 in Upper Canada and none since Confederation in Canada; and no motion in either House or movement in that direction has ever been made.

[7]The two final appellate tribunals for the British world, are (1) the House of Lords for England, Scotland and Ireland and (2) the Judicial Committee of the Privy Council for the remainder. This Committee is technically not a Court (it does not give judgments, but advice to the Sovereign); but for all practical purposes it is a Court. The members of the Committee are from the British Islands and the self-governing Dominions and India. See my Address to the Missouri Bar Association, Sept. 17, 1904; Bentwich's Privy Council, London, 1912. Most, if not all, of the Law Lords of the House of Lords are members as well of the Judicial Committee.

A very small number of cases are taken to the Judicial Committee from Canada, but these are generally of great importance. The Judicial Committee has had much to do with keeping the jurisprudence of the various British peoples uniform; it is a consummation which I think is devoutly to be wished that all communities under the Common Law should have uniform jurisprudence.

From the Reports, the following is the number of cases reported from Canada as heard by the Committee in 1921–1922. There were a very few not reported:

PROVINCE	NO. IN 1921	NO. IN 1922
Ontario	1	0
Quebec	10	4
Nova Scotia	0	0
New Brunswick	0	0
Prince Edward Island	0	0
Manitoba	0	1
Saskatchewan	0	0
Alberta	0	1
British Columbia and Yukon Territory	3	4
General	0	2
TOTAL	14	12

[8]B. N. A. Act, sec. 92, (8).

[9]One of the Lieutenant-Governors of Upper Canada in the days before Responsible Government characterized the Municipal Councils as "Sucking Republics."

[10] Indirectly it had some influence—the French Canadian prevented any provision for the Dominion amending its written Constitution, the B. N. A. Act, 1867.

[11] This and many other documents of importance will be found printed in "Documents relating to the Constitutional History of Canada, 1759-1791," edited by Drs. Shortt and Doughty, and issued by the Canadian Archives. The second and much improved edition was printed by the King's Printer at Ottawa, 1918. This most admirable collection will be quoted as "S. & D."

The Treaty of Paris is at S & D, pp. 97, 113, sqq.

[12] The Régime Militaire in fact continued until the establishment of the Civil Courts, September 17, 1764; but some consider that it came to an end on the issue of the Royal Proclamation of October 7, 1763—it is a mere matter of terminology and not worth discussing.

[23] For the Royal Proclamation of October 7, 1763, see S & D, 163, Murray's Commission, do., p. 173, Royal Institutions, do., p. 181; Ordinance of September 17, 1764, do., p. 205. The Proclamation promised the English Laws, Civil and Criminal; while the English Criminal law, was thus introduced, the English Civil law was so only partially—the matter is obscure and uncertain in some regards, and I do not here discuss it.

[14] For the first time since the Reformation, in British Territory, perfect religious tolerance and equality were established in Quebec by the Quebec Act (1774) 14 Geo. III., C. 83, (Imp.). It will be remembered that this toleration of Roman Catholics roused the fiercest indignation of the Continental Congress at Philadelphia who could not suppress their astonishment that a British Parliament should establish in Canada "a religion that has deluged your Island in blood and dispersed impiety, bigotry, persecution, murder and rebellion through every part of the world."

[15] For the Quebec Act, (1774), 14 Geo. III., C. 83, (Imp.), see S & D, p. 570. A considerable part of the discussion, petitions, resolutions, etc., leading up to the passing of the Canada or Constitutional Act of 1791 will be found in these volumes.

[16] (1791), 31 Geo. III., C. 31, (Imp.), see S & D, p. 1031. The boundaries of Upper and Lower Canada respectively were practically the same as those of the Provinces of Ontario and Quebec in 1867.

The Order-in-Council dividing the former Province of Quebec into Upper Canada and Lower Canada was passed August 24, 1791; it is to be found in "Documents relating to the Constitutional History of Canada, 1791–1818" edited by Doughty and McArthur, printed by the King's Printer, Ottawa 1914, at p. 3.

[17] There was a Governor-in-Chief who generally resided at Quebec and acted as Governor of Lower Canada: also a Lieutenant-Governor of Upper Canada whose powers in Upper Canada were the same as those of the Governor-in-Chief when the Governor-in-Chief was not in the Province—and also a Lieutenant-Governor of Lower Canada with the same powers there when the Governor-in-Chief was absent. The language of the Canada Act which I abbreviate by using the word "Governor" alone, is "Governor or Lieutenant-Governor or person administering the Government in each of the said Provinces respectively."

[18] During this period, the usual practice after the first Councillors, was for the Governor to recommend a person as Legislative Councillor; and this recommendation was generally approved by the Home Administration who sent out to the Colony a Mandamus or Warrant to swear in the nominee.

[19] The same terminology as in the B. N. A. Act; but with a world of difference in connotation.

[20] Bills for Divorce were reserved for the Queen's pleasure till 1878 when the Instructions were changed in this particular as in others.

[21] The Legislative Council and Assembly in Lower Canada were suspended for more than two years till November 1, 1840; and temporary provision made for the government of and legislation for the Province by a Special Council appointed by the Home Administration. (1838) 1, 2 Vict., C. 9 (Imp.).

No such provision was necessary in Upper Canada, where the population was generally loyal and the Rebellion was put down almost immediately.

[22] (1840) 3, 4 Vict., C. 35 (Imp.).

[23] It was the day of small things, but one statesman at least had a glimpse of the real significance of the gathering. Lord Salisbury said:—

"We all feel the gravity and importance of this occasion. The decisions of this Conference may not be for the moment, of vital importance; the business may seem prosaic, and may not issue in any great results at the moment. But we are all sensible that this meeting is the beginning of a state of things which is to have great results in the future. It will be the parent of a long progeniture, and distant councils of the Empire may, in some far-off time, look back to the meeting in this room as the root from which all their greatness and all their beneficence sprang."

[24] See Chapter II, note 32, p. 32, *supra*.

[25] This was formed pursuant to the following Resolution of the Colonial Council:

"That it will be to the advantage of the Empire if a conference, to be called the Imperial Conference, is held every four years, at which questions of common interest may be discussed and considered as between His Majesty's Government and His Governments of the Self-Governing Dominions beyond the seas.

The Prime Minister of the United Kingdom will be ex-officio President, and the Prime Minister of the self-governing Dominions will be ex-officio members of the Conference. The Secretary of State for the Colonies will be ex-officio member of the Conference and will take the chair in the absence of the President. He will arrange for such Imperial Conference after communication with the Prime Ministers of the respective Dominions."

Almost immediately, Canada began to form a Navy of her own.

[26] Curiously enough the terminology is still in vogue in the United States.

[27] The language of the President of the Council at Ottawa in his place in the House of Commons.

The Imperial War Cabinet itself says in the Official Report for 1918:

"The common effort and sacrifice in the war have inevitably led to the recognition of an equality of status between the responsible governments of the Empire. This equality has long been acknowledged in principle, and found its adequate expression in 1917 in the creation, or rather, natural coming into being, of an Imperial War Cabinet as an instrument for evolving a common Imperial policy in the conduct of the war. The nature of the constitutional development involved in the establishment as a permanent institution of the Imperial Cabinet system was clearly explained by Sir Robert Borden in a speech to the Empire Parliamentary Association on the 21st of June, 1918."

What the Prime Minister, Sir Robert Borden, said at the meeting of the Imperial Council is as follows:

"A very great step in the constitutional development of the Empire was taken last year by the Prime Minister when he summoned the Prime Ministers of the Overseas Dominions to the Imperial War Cabinet. We met there on terms of perfect equality. We met there as Prime Ministers of self-governing nations. We met there under the leadership and the presidency of the Prime Minister of the United Kingdom. After all, my Lord Chancellor and gentlemen, the British Empire, as it is at present constituted, is a very modern organization. It is perfectly true that is is built up on the development of centuries, but as it is constituted today, both in territory and in organization, it is a relatively modern affair. Why, it is only 75 years since Responsible Government was granted to Canada. It is only little more than fifty years since the first experiment in Federal Government,—in a Federal Constitution,—was undertaken in this Empire. And from that we went on, in 1871, to representation in negotiating our commercial treaties; in 1878 to complete fiscal autonomy, and after that to complete fiscal control and the negotiations of our own treaties. But we have always lacked the full status of nationhood because you exercised here [i. e., in England] a so-called trusteeship under which you undertook to deal with foreign relations on our behalf, and sometimes without consulting us very much. Well, that day has gone by. We come here, as we came last year, to deal with all these matters, upon terms of perfect equality with the Prime Minister of the United Kingdom and his colleagues.

Every Prime Minister who sits round that board is responsible to his own Parliament and to his own people; the conclusions of the War Cabinet can only be carried out by the Parliaments of the different nations of our Imperia Commonwealth. Thus each dominion, each nation, retains its perfect autonomy. I venture to believe, and I thus expressed myself last year, that in this may be found the genesis of a development in the constitutional relation of the Empire which will form the basis of its unity in the years to come."

[28] There are those who see or affect to see in this a deep-laid scheme to give Britain an advantage over other nations. There is no scheme, no plot; it was not the United Kingdom who desired the presence of the Dominions at the Treaty Council table and in the League of Nations—the Dominions themselves demanded it as a right and as in accord with the fact. I more than doubt that the United Kingdom will receive any advantage from their presence at either—so far the evidence is the other way. Ask some of the

European countries what they think of Canada's stand concerning natural resources; nay, ask the British statesmen themselves, what they think of Canada's demand for the excision of Article X, which we protested against in the beginning, protested against again at Geneva, and which we may continue to protest against until it disappears.

However that may be, in the absence of the British Dominions there can be no really international conference, and we will not, to please any nation, change our attitude. We will not go back to the colonial status, and to give up our flag is too high a price to pay—we will not pay it. If any other nation stay out of the League, that is its business, not ours; we do not criticize or complain; we are in and we stay in as along as it pleases us.

It has been suggested that we should have an Ambassador at Washington. The official statement reads thus:

"As a result of recent discussions, an arrangement has been concluded between the British and Canadian Governments to provide more complete representation of Canadian interests at Washington than has hitherto existed. Accordingly it has been agreed that His Majesty, on the advice of his Canadian Ministers, shall appoint a Minister Plenipotentiary, who will have charge of Canadian affairs and will at all times be the ordinary channel of communication with the United States Government in matters of purely Canadian concern, acting upon instructions from and reporting direct to the Canadian Government.

In the absence of the Ambassador, the Canadian Minister will take charge of the whole Embassy and of the representation of Imperial as well as Canadian interests. He will be accredited by His Majesty to the President with necessary powers for the purpose. This new arrangement will not denote any departure either on the part of the British Government or the Canadian Government from the principle of the diplomatic unity of the British Empire.

The need for this important step has been fully realized by both Governments for some time. For a good many years there has been direct communication between Ottawa and Washington, but the constantly increasing importance of Canadian interests in the United States has made it apparent that in addition Canada should be represented there in some distinctive manner, for this would doubtless tend to expedite negotiations and, naturally, first-hand acquaintance with Canadian conditions would promote good understanding.

In view of the peculiarly close relations that have existed between the people of Canada and those of the United States, it is confidently expected as well that this new step will have the desirable result of maintaining and strengthening the friendly relations and co-operation between the British Empire and the United States."

This project hangs fire for the present for various reasons, but it will in any case be a Canadian question for Canadians to decide as they think wise. Moreover it is but putting in regular form what has (so far as Canada is concerned) long been the practice.

We made an arrangement with the United States in 1903 and 1905 for a

Joint Board of Commissioners to deal with International waters; in 1909 we made a Treaty for the present International Joint Commission. After the abrogation of the Reciprocity Treaty in 1866, we many times sent envoys from Canada to Washington to obtain if possible a new Reciprocity Treaty, and when the time seemed auspicious in 1911, we sent representatives— Ambassadors in all but name—to negotiate a new Treaty. We in fact deal and have for years dealt directly with the American authorities; and the new scheme is but a change in form.

Even as I write, there is announced the signing of a Convention between the United States and Canada for the preservation of the Halibut Fisheries of the Northern Pacific which are being rapidly depleted—this Convention was negotiated by Canadians direct and without the intervention of the Ambassador of Britain.

[29] I should do Britain a gross wrong if I were to leave the impression that the self-government of Canada was wrung from her in her despite—the reverse is the fact. There have been some reactionaries on both sides of the Atlantic; but on the whole, Britain has gladly and readily given Canada from time to time such proportion of self-government as she desired: most of the objection to change came from Canadians, and the Rebellion of 1837-8 was at least in Upper Canada a Rebellion against Canadian misrule, not against British interference.

The heartfelt desire of Britain has always been for Canadian happiness. She knew that people of our race cannot be happy unless they govern themselves, whether for weal or for woe—there was never to be a second Bunker Hill.

It should also be said that from the earliest Colonial times in Canada, any and every modification in her status has been viewed with apprehension by many Canadians wholly sincere, thoughtful and patriotic. They looked upon every change as tending to loosen the ties which bound Canada to the Mother Country—sometimes as leading to annexation. The reverse has proved to be the fact: no change has diminished in any the slightest degree, the loyalty of Canada to British connection and her determination to remain part of the British Commonwealth. Her loyalty to the Crown was never greater than it is today when the aspirations of the United Empire Loyalists for perfect freedom under the British Flag have been completely realized. The cardinal error in the old British Empire was that the Colonies were considered as fruit to be plucked not as branches incorporated in and part of the mother tree. As Turgot prophesied, thus treated, "Colonies . . . cling to the tree only till they ripen. . . . As soon as America can take care of herself, she will do what Carthage did."

The old British Empire received its deathblow on this Continent from the American separation: the new and greater British Empire finds its greatest strength in Canadian loyalty.

Esto perpetua.

INDEX

Abbott, Sir John J. C., Prime Minister of Canada, 42
Alberta, Province of
formed (1905), 6; unicameral, 25
Ambassador to United States, 23, 32, 69
Amendments to Constitution
of Dominion
why not provided for in B. N. A. Act, 3
how made, 3
list of, 9, 10
of Provinces
provision for in B. N. A. Act, 4
examples of, 4, 10
exception, 4, 11

Blackstone's Commentaries
quoted, 5, 12
Blake, Edward
Prime Minister of Ontario, 41
Minister of Justice of Canada, 27
Borden, Sir Robert Laird
Prime Minister of Canada, 29, 40, 42
Statement at Imperial Council, 68
his "Canadian Historical Studies", viii
de Boucherville, M., Prime Minister of Quebec, 45
Bracken, John
Prime Minister of Manitoba, 26
British Columbia, Province of
enters Dominion (1871), 6
abolishes Second Chamber, 10, 25
British Connection
Canadian sentiment as to, 70
British North America Act, 1867
written Constitution of Canada, 1
origin, 1; a treaty, 8
amendments to, how made, 2, 9, 10

"British Preference," 32, 61
Brown, George
Commissioner at Washington (1874), 31
victim of "Double Shuffle," 27, 43
Leader of Reform Party, 42

"Cabinet," *see* Ministry
Canada
geographical composition of, 1
Cartwright, Sir Richard
on Joint High Commission, 31
Cases cited
British
City of London *v.* Wood (1700), 12 Mod., 669, 12
Bank of Australasia *v.* Noris (1857), 16 Q. B., 717, 30
The Queen *v.* Burah (1878), 3 A. C., 889, 11, 14
Hodge *v.* The Queen (1883), 9 A. C., 117, 11, 15
Powell *v.* Apollo Candle Company (1885), 10 A. C., 282, 11
Royal Bank of Canada *v.* Rex (1913), A. C., 283, 14
re Initiative and Referendum Act (1919), A. C., 935, 10
Canadian
Regina *v.* J. Kerr (1838), 2 N. B. Rep., 367, 558, 30
McDonell *v.* Smith (1859), 17 U. C., Q. B., 310, 43
Macdonell *v.* Macdonald (1859), 8 U. C., C. P., 479, 43
re Goodhue (1872), Grant Ch. R. 366, 15
Rex *v.* Hodge (1882), 46 U. C., Q. B., 141, 15
Delamatter *v.* Brown (1908), 13 O. W. R. 58, 15
Florence M. Co. *v.* Cobalt M.

Co. (1908), 18 O. L. R. 275, 12, 14. S. C. in Judicial Com. (1910), 43 O. L. R. 474; 102 L. T., N. S., 375, 12

Smith *v.* City of London (1909), 20 O. L. R., 11, 15

Royal Bank of Canada *v.* Rex (1912), 4 Alta. L. R., 249, 2, 14

Bell *v.* Town of Burlington (1915), 34 O. L. R., 619, 7

re Initiative and Referendum Act (1916), 27 Man. L. R., 1, 10

re Hammond Will (1921), 21 O. W. N., 100, 184; 51 O. L. R., 149, 15

Manitoba F. P. Co. *v.* Fort Francis P. & P. Co. (1922), 22 O. W. N., 56, 277, 14

re Hill *v.* Glenwood Nat. Gas Co. (1923), 14

Clemency of Crown
how exercised, 27, 28

Colonial Conference
formed (1887), 60
Lord Salisbury's view of, 68
termination of (1907), 61, 67

Commissioners, powers delegated to, 6, 14, 15

Commons, House of
composition, 18
election of members, 18, 33
resignation of members, 39, 40
Ministry responsible to, 19, 21
Money-Bills in, 36, 46, 49
Speaker elected by House, 25

Conflict of legislative authority, 39

"Constitution"
meaning of, 1, 7, 16
written, of Canada, 2; historical sketch, 55–63

Constitution of United States referred to, 1, 4, 5, 7, 10, 19, 26, 39

"Constitutional Limitations"
none in Canada, 5, 6

Davies, Sir Louis (now Chief Justice of Canada)
on Joint High Commission, 31

"Delegates non potest delegare"
no application to Canadian legislation, 4, 5, 14

Disallowance of legislation
Dominion, 37, 38
Provincial, 29, 38, 47, 48

"Dominion"
origin of name, 8
reason for adoption, 8
present connotation, 62

"Double Shuffle," 27, 63

Drury, Ernest C.
Prime Minister of Ontario (1920), 41, 43

Election
General
what, 33
when and why held, 33, 34, 35
in Dominion, list of, 40, 41, 42
in Province of Ontario, list of, 41, 42, 43
By-election
what, 33

Electoral College (U. S.)
in theory and in fact, 7, 26

Electoral Franchise, *see* Franchise

"Eminent Domain"
none in Canada, 15

Exchequer Court of Canada
erected, 53 63, 64

"Exclusive," "Exclusively"
meaning of, in B. N. A. Act, 14

Executive—nominally the Sovereign, 17

Ex post facto legislation valid, 16

Fenian Raids (1866, 1867), 8, 9

Ferguson, G. Howard
Prime Minister of Ontario (1923), 41, 43

Foreign Relations, 23

Franchise, electoral
in Dominion, 18, 26

in Provinces, 19
in Yukon Territory, 49

Galt, Sir Alexander Tulloch
negotiated with Spain and France, 32
Gibbons, Sir George
Commissioner at Washington, 31
"Government Bills"
what: effect of defeating, 20, 21, 26
Governor-General
represents the King, 17, 22
and monarchical principle, 26
how appointed, 22
may be recalled, 43, 44
responsible to Imperial Government, 35
principles governing conduct, 34, 35
not responsible to House of Commons, 21
must sometimes exercise personal judgment, 34
salary, 46
Governors-General mentioned
Former Province of Canada
Sir Edmund Head, 43
Dominion of Canada
Lord Dufferin, 30, 42, 44
Marquis of Lorne, 27, 44
Earl of Aberdeen, 28

Halibut Fisheries Convention (1923), 70
Hardy, Arthur Sturgis
Prime Minister of Ontario, 41, 42
Hearst, Sir William H.
Prime Minister of Ontario, 41, 42
Historical Sketch of Constitution of Canada, 55-63
House of Commons. See Commons, House of
Hudson Bay Company
sold Rupert's Land to Canada, 8

Imperial Conference
formed (1907), 61, 68

Imperial War Cabinet, 29, 67, 68
Initiative and Referendum Act
(Manitoba), held *ultra vires*, 4, 11

Joly, M.
Prime Minister of Quebec, 44, 45
Judges
appointment of, 53
tenure of office, 54
removal of, 65
Barristers, 64
Judicial Committee of the Privy Council
final Court of Appeal, 65
cases in, 65
Jurisdiction in Legislation
of Dominion, 5, 11, 12, 13
of Provinces, 5, 11, 14, 15
of Yukon Territory, 50
of North West Territories, 51, 52
of Imperial Parliament, 14, 22, 23, 28, 29

King, nominal Executive, 17
represented by Governor-General, 22
or Lieutenant-Governor, 4, 17
never in Canada, 17, 24
King, William Lyon Mackenzie
Prime Minister of Canada (1922), 40, 42

Laurier, Sir Wilfrid
Prime Minister of Canada, 31, 32, 40, 41, 42
League of Nations
Canada, a member of, 61
Legislation
responsibility for, 21, 22
money-bills, 36
Royal Assent, 37, 38
disallowance (Dominion) 37, 38;
(Provincial), 38, 47, 48
form of legislation, 48, 49
Legislative Council, *see* Second Chamber

Legislative powers
not delegated, 4, 5
Legislature of Province
bicameral in Quebec and New
Brunswick, 18, 25
unicameral in Nova Scotia, Prince
Edward Island, Ontario, Manitoba, Saskatchewan, Alberta and
British Columbia, 18, 25
term of, 33; self-extended, 10
election, 19, 33
members' resignation, 40
Letellier, Luc, Lieutenant-Governor
of Quebec removed, 44, 45
Lieutenant-Governor
represents King, 4, 17
rights and duties quâ elections,
etc., 35
responsible to Governor-General,
35
term of office, 36
removal of, 36
reasons for, 36
instance of removal, 44, 45
Lieutenant-Governors mentioned
Manitoba
Sir Douglas Cameron, 45
Sir James Aikins, 27
Quebec
Luc Letellier
dismisses Ministry and is removed, 44, 45
M. Angers
dismisses Ministry and is
sustained, 45

Manitoba
formed, 6
abolishes Second Chamber, 25
Initiative and Referendum Act, 4,
11
Manitoba School Question Election
(1896), 40, 42
Ministry
what, 19, 20, 21
how formed, 19
when must resign, 19, 20, 21

responsible to House of Commons,
21, 45
not to Governor-General, 21
must have seat in Parliament, 22
joint responsibility, 21, 22
dismissal of, 44, 45
Meighen, Arthur
Prime Minister of Canada, 40, 42
Mercier, M., Prime Minister of
Quebec
dismissed from office, 45
Monarchical System assured, 3, 4, 26
Governor-General representative
of, 26
Money Bills
how and where introduced, 36, 49
practice as to, 46
Mowat, Sir Oliver
Prime Minister of Ontario, 41, 42
Municipal System, 54
"Suckling Republics," 65
Macdonald, Sir John Alexander
Prime Minister of Canada, 30, 40
Plenipotentiary at Washington
(1871), 31
Macdonald, John Sandfield
Prime Minister of Ontario, 42
Mackenzie, Alexander
Prime Minister of Canada, 40, 42

"National Policy Election" (1878),
40, 42
New Brunswick
original Province of Dominion
(1867), 1, 6
abolishes Second Chamber, 10
Newfoundland
a party to Confederation Conference, 1
declined to enter Dominion, 1
legislation extending term of
legislature, 10
"North East" Boundary, 31
North West Territories, 1, 7
legislature, 51, 52
Nova Scotia
original Province of Dominion, 1, 6

bicameral, 10, 25
Ontario
original Province of Dominion (1867), 6
unicameral, 25
elections and Prime Ministers, 41, 42, 43

"Pacific Scandal" Election, 40, 42
Parliament of Canada
composition, 17
term, 33; extended, 10
jurisdiction, 5, 12, 13
Prime Minister or Premier
what, 19
list of (Dominion), 40; (Ontario), 41
Prince Edward Island
a party to Confederation Conference, 1
declined to enter Dominion, 1
became a Province of Canada (1873), 6
abolished Second Chamber, 10, 35
Privy Council of Canada, 19, 20
Privy Council (Imperial), Judicial Committee of, 54, 65
Protective Tariff
an issue in Dominion Election of 1878, 40, 42
Provinces of Canada
original, 6
added, 6
Legislatures of, 18, 25, 33, 40
jurisdiction of, 5, 14, 15

Quebec
original Province of Dominion (1867), 6
bicameral, 25
former Province of, 55
dismissal of Provincial Ministry in, 44, 45
"Roberts Case" in, 16
"Quebec Conference," 2

"Reciprocity Election" (1911), 25, 40, 41, 42

Reciprocity Treaty (1854), 7, 31; (1911), 25, 31, 40, 41, 42
Residue of legislative power in Dominion, 5
"Responsible Government"
what, 19
"Roberts Case" in Quebec, 16
Ross, Sir George, W. 10
Prime Minister of Ontario, 41, 42
Rupert's Land
bought from Hudson Bay Company, 8
legislation concerning, validated, 9

Saskatchewan
formed, 6
unicameral, 25
Second Chamber
abolished, 4, 10, 25
Senate
composition, 17, 24; increase provided for, 24
members, how appointed, 18
Speaker of, 18, 25; Deputy-Speaker, 9
Smith, Professor Goldwin
dissatisfied with sovereign powers of Legislature, 14
Statutes referred to. See list at end of Index
Supreme Court of Canada
erected, 53, 63, 64
jurisdiction in Constitutional Questions, 30
Supreme Court of Ontario
jurisdiction in Constitutional Questions, 30, 31

Territories of Canada, 1. See North West Territories and Yukon Territory
Thompson, Sir John S. D.
Prime Minister of Canada, 42
"Thou shalt not steal"
not of force to Legislatures, 14
Treaties
of Paris (1763), 55, 56

Jay's (1794), 6
Washington (1871), 31
Bering Sea (1892), 31
"Trent Affair"
   referred to, 7
Tupper, Sir Charles
   Prime Minister of Canada, 42
   Plenipotentiary in Atlantic Fish-
      eries negotiations, 31
   negotiated Treaty with France, 32
Tupper, Sir Charles Hibbert
   negotiated Bering Sea Treaty
      (1892), 31

Unicameral Provinces, 25
United States
   relations with, 23, 70

Whitney, Sir James Pliny
   Prime Minister of Ontario, 41, 42
Wills, powers of Legislatures to vary,
      15, 16

Yukon Territory
   history, 6, 7
   government of, 49, 50, 51

STATUTES REFERRED TO

Note. In our system, Statutes are cited by reference to the regnant year of the Sovereign and Chapter, thus "34 Geo. III, C. 31" means the 31st Chapter of the legislation of the Parliament in the 34th year of the reign of George III. The contractions (Imp.), (Can.), (Dom.), (Ont.) etc. are added to show what Parliament passed the legislation, Imperial, that of the former Province of Canada, of the Dominion, of the Province of Ontario, etc.

        Imperial   (Imp.)
1553   25 Henry VIII, C. 20, 26
1705   4, 5 Anne, C. 20, 27
1715   1 Geo. I, Stat. 2, C. 38, 10

1774   14 Geo. III, C. 83 (the Que-
           bec Act), 6, 57, 66
1791   31 Geo. III, C. 31 (the Can-
           ada or Constitutional Act),
           6, 58, 66
1838   1, 2 Vict., C. 9, 67
1840   3, 4 Vict., C. 35 (the Union
           Act), 3, 6, 8, 60, 67
1861   24, 25 Vict., C. 67, 11
1865   28, 29 Vict., C. 63, 28, 30
1866   29, 30 Vict., C. 67, 6
1867   30, 31 Vict., C. 3 (B. N. A.
           Act), passim
1869   32, 33 Vict., C. 101, 8
1870   33, 34 Vict., C. 82, 9
1871   34 Vict., C. 28, 9
1875   38, 39 Vict., C. 38, 9
1892   55, 56 Vict., C. 82, 9
1895   59 Vict., C. 3, 9
1907   7 Edw. VII, C. 11, 9
1911   1, 2 Geo. V, C. 13, 10
1912   2, 3 Geo. V, C. 10, 29
1915   5, 6 Geo. V, C. 45, 10, 25;
           C. 100, 11
1916   6, 7 Geo. V, C. 19, 10: C. 100,
           11
1917   7 Geo. V, C. 13, 11

Former Province of Canada (Can.)

1849   12 Vict., C. 63, 64
1857   20 Vict., C. 22, 43; C. 58, 64
1859   C. S. U. C., C. 14, 64

      Dominion of Canada (Dom.)

1870   33 Vict., C. 3, 24
1875   38 Vict., C. 11, 63
1887   50, 51 Vict., C. 16, 64
           R. S. Can., C. 53, 7
1894   57, 58 Vict., C. 11, 9
1898   61 Vict., C. 6, 7
1905   4, 5 Edw. VII, C. 3, 24; C. 27,
           7; C. 42, 24
1906   R. S. Can., C. 10, 27; C. 11,
           39, 40; C. 48, 26; C. 62, 7;
           C. 139, 30
1914   4, 5 Geo. V, C. 51, 25

1920   10, 11 Geo. V, C. 26, 64

Province of Ontario (Ont.)

1914   R. S. O., C. 5, 25, 26; C. 11,
         40; C. 56, 14; C. 57, 64;
         C. 85, 30
1916   6 Geo. V, C. 3, 15
1917   7 Geo. V, C. 27, 15
1918   8 Geo. V, C. 4, 10
1919   9 Geo. V, C. 25, 15
1920   10, 11 Geo. V, C. 29, 15
1921   11 Geo. V, C. 17, 15

Province of Alberta (Alta.)

(1917)   C. 38, 11
(1922)   R. S. Alta., C. 3, 26

Province of Manitoba (Man.)

1913   R. S. Man. C. 25, 26
1916   6 Geo. V, C. 59, 11

Province of Saskatchewan (Sask.)

1920   R. S. Sask., C. 2, 26

Newfoundland (Nfld.)

1918   8, 9 Geo. V, C. 2, 10

Province of New Brunswick (N. B.)

(1903)   R. S. N. B., C. 3, 26

Province of Prince Edward Island (P. E. I.)

(1913)   Acts P. E. I., C. 1, 26

www.ingramcontent.com/pod-product-compliance
Lightning Source LLC
LaVergne TN
LVHW091229080426
835509LV00009B/1224